Backyard Carolina
Two Decades of Public Radio Commentary

Summer 2017
For Cathe & Rick,
   with thanks for joining me
on the Black River!

AnDy

BACKYARD CAROLINA

Two Decades of Public Radio Commentary

Andy Wood

EDITED BY LOUISA JONAS
ILLUSTRATIONS BY MELISSA SMITH

Backyard Carolina: Two Decades of Public Radio Commentary
© 2006 University of North Carolina Wilmington

Edited by Louisa Jonas
Illustrated by Melissa Smith
Book design and cover by Emily Smith
Editorial assistants: Gwendolyn Knapp, Sumanth Prabhaker
Publishing Laboratory faculty: Barbara Brannon, Robert Siegel

FRONT COVER Spotted turtle, bald cypress, and pine lily photographs by Andy Wood for Audubon North Carolina; great egret by Randy Newman for the North Carolina Division of Parks and Recreation; used by permission.

Printed in the United States of America
09 08 07   5 4 3 2
ISBN-13 978-0-9719308-8-9
ISBN-10 0-9719308-8-0

LIBRARY OF CONGRESS CATALOGUING-IN-PUBLICATION DATA
Wood, Andy, 1955 –
Backyard Carolina : two decades of public radio commentary /
Andy Wood ; edited by Louisa Jonas ; illustrations by Melissa Smith.
p. cm.
ISBN-13: 978-0-9719308-8-9
1. Natural history — North Carolina. I. Jonas, Louisa. II. Title.
QH105.N8W66 2006
508.756 — dc22
2006016904

THE
PUBLISHING
LABORATORY
UNIVERSITY OF NORTH CAROLINA WILMINGTON

Published by The Publishing Laboratory
Department of Creative Writing
University of North Carolina Wilmington
601 South College Road
Wilmington, North Carolina 28403 USA
www.uncw.edu/writers

This book is lovingly dedicated to my closest friends: Sandy, Robin, and Carson (and P. magnifica).

CONTENTS

3 | Beyond All That

ILLUSTRATIONS

Preface

WHEN I ASK MYSELF "WHAT IS BACKYARD CAROLINA?" I first think it is a journal spanning nearly twenty years, a diary that I read aloud on public radio station WHQR, broadcast out of Wilmington, North Carolina. It is a compilation of observations in nature from my own back yard to the larger back yard of various communities in southeastern North Carolina and northeastern South Carolina. And like a diary, many of these written observations include my inner feelings and thoughts regarding the health and well-being of our home, this place we call Earth.

If there is a unifying thread in this book/journal it is my unwavering belief that people need to connect with the natural world that supports and sustains them. We are not alone on this planet, and we have much to learn from the nonhuman members of our communities, including the plants and animals that help keep this place so dynamic.

These essays might try to coax you out of doors, even if only into your back yard or neighborhood park. Once you're outside, I hope you will take time to observe the wonders of nature that abound all around us, from little ants to giant woodpeckers. We need not travel to far-flung corners of the globe to discover nature's glory: nature, the lessons she can teach, the resources she provides, the enlightenment she inspires, and the joy she evokes, is in truth right outside our doors.

During the two decades that these passages represent, I charged myself with the responsibility to make my observations and comments relevant and meaningful to my radio audience. I am very grateful to this audience because were it not for their attention and encouragement over the years, I might not have persisted in this labor of love.

Of course, I must thank WHQR and the family of staff members who helped me through the years with edits and recording. Jim Polson, Aileen LeBlanc, George Scheibner, and Scott Simpson are due thanks for their forbearance with me as each one tried, with mixed success, to teach me the finer points of audio recording technology and radio delivery.

The long hours the radio staff endured are but a fraction of the time my wife, Sandy, and our two sons, Robin and Carson, permitted me as I wrote, edited, and then recorded each piece. I trust the reader will see that my family is as much a part of this work as are the subjects of nature herein described.

I am thankful to my mother, Janet, for allowing me to wander the woods and bring home whatever living thing I found (and for removing the small beings from my pockets before going to the laundry). I am grateful to my father, G. Congdon Wood, for my innate curiosity about nature (and a love of beetles). He passed on to me a heritage that, with my sons, now spans at least five generations. Thanks are also due to my ever-patient stepfather, Robert Fairlie, who taught me the finer arts of cage crafting (maybe to assure himself that my snakes would stay kept); and to my stepmother, Bari Wood, who helped convince me to pursue a career as an environmental educator.

Were it not for my brothers Chris, Jon, and David and my late brother Gil, I might never have come to appreciate the subtle differences between the foul flavor of toad and the acrid taste of millipede. They also helped prepare me for the trouble I might get into, when—not if—any of my animals escaped inside the house. Special thanks are due to my brother Jon, for his encouragement and help during the several years that this book has been in the making, including transcribing my early handwritten pieces to type so that this work could proceed.

During much of my tenure as a radio commentator, I served as education curator with the North Carolina Aquarium at Fort Fisher, where I learned the true sense of "form follows function," along with the skills required to collect live sharks while I was extremely seasick. It was also through this institution that I became connected with the wonderful world of marine educators: the Mid-Atlantic Marine Education Association and the National Marine Educators Association.

The reader will see that I have much to say about birds. This is because, like millions of other nature lovers, I am quite fond of birds, and it is by good fortune that I now work for the North Carolina office of the National Audubon Society, one of our nation's oldest and most highly respected conservation organizations. I am very glad that my father lived long enough to see me move in with this dedicated group of like-minded conservationists.

Additional thanks go to Louisa Jonas and the team of UNCW Publishing Laboratory editors for the great editing they performed; whittling hundreds of commentaries down to fifty-two took stamina and perseverance. And thanks also to Melissa Smith for her masterful artworks representing some of my most beloved critters, and to Emily Smith for designing all this into something readable. I am especially grateful to Barbara Brannon, director of the Publishing Laboratory, and to UNCW for enabling all of us to work on this team effort.

Oops—I almost forgot one other. I am certain I shall never meet so wonderful a creature as the magnificent rams-horn snail. To know *Planorbella magnifica* has been one of my life's greatest joys, and maybe one day I will write a book about this humble being. As friends have noted, I am fascinated with what some might consider mundane. Read on and you will hopefully understand why.

Andy Wood

Introduction

ANDY WOOD HAS AN UNYIELDING CURIOSITY about the outdoors. As radio commentator, naturalist, and environmental educator, he has dedicated his life to sharing with others his enthusiasm for nature. On the air, Andy's voice is a friendly one; it reaches any listener who wants a good laugh and is interested in the world. For twenty years, Andy's radio commentaries have provided a rich resource to a wide range of people who share his concerns for the environment and his sense of wonder with nature. Andy has never intended his commentaries to reach only "nature people" (whatever that means), scientists, or naturalists, though he himself is one of them.

Andy is as inclusive toward his subject matter as he is toward his audience. He pays rapt attention to both ordinary and extraordinary events in the coastal plains of the Carolinas, and sometimes beyond. Pitcher plants, flying squirrels, and loggerhead turtles do not always confine themselves to state lines—and neither does Andy. He speaks of what he discovers on the land, in the sea, and in the sky, where and when he discovers them.

His stories have left their mark. People stop Andy in the grocery store, recognize his baritone voice, and share in wistful tones how they find themselves thinking about the common loon he saved. They tell him how they laughed at the snapping turtle fiasco or that they'll never look at a puddle the same way again. Recently they've been saying, "When are you going to come out with a book?"

In the fall of 2004, the Publishing Laboratory, the publishing arm of the University of North Carolina Wilmington, sought proposals for regional book projects serving the southeastern states. I had known Andy a short while when I first heard his commentary on local public radio station WHQR 91.3; a collection of these commentaries seemed an obvious fit. I met Andy the previous summer on Wrightsville Beach, where he had led a public talk about the need to protect bird-nesting sanctuaries. Standing next to the roped-off sanctuary site under a brutal August sun, Andy gestured wildly at the mottled shorebird eggs camouflaged amid shell hash and sand on the other side of the rope. He explained that camouflage is a brilliant strategy to avoid the attention of foxes and other ground predators. When such areas are not protected, however, even the most careful person can't decipher egg from shell and unknowingly steps on the eggs.

The attendees nodded, squinted under floppy hats, searching for the eggs amidst the sand and shells. They forgot about the summer heat. In person and on the radio, Andy's enthusiasm is contagious. His observations and stories are too good not to live on the page.

It has not been easy to narrow down two decades of radio commentary to fifty-two selections. A type of history unfolds when reading weekly commentaries that span twenty years. Andy was on the air for the infamous *Exxon Valdez* oil spill of 1989, and he was on the air in September 2001, days after the twin towers fell. Though the editorial team briefly considered selecting commentaries from each year and laying the book out temporally, the idea was quickly discarded. Andy's intent has not been to chronicle the passage of time, but rather to take notice and often celebrate what is alive in the here and now.

In the end we selected what we considered the best of the best. Andy tells funny stories and sad stories; some commentaries educate, some call us to action, and others make us stop and think. We have tried to represent a little of it all. Andy asks nothing of his listeners and readers that he does not ask of himself. For the most part, though, you'll find in these pages the musings of a naturalist as he joyfully discovers his world. There is no hard-line agenda here.

Though the traditional nature collection is arranged seasonally, we have chosen a format that we believe collectively tells a bigger picture. We wanted to remain true to what we thought was the most interesting arrangement, while recognizing the practicality of a seasonal approach. We hope the thematically ordered commentaries will guide the reader whose interest is to read cover to cover. And we hope that the seasonal progression within each section will easily serve the reader who, say, in February wants to help feed the woodpeckers and warblers, and in June tries to decipher a skink from an anole.

Stories are told differently when they are spoken out loud than when they are written for the page. The immediacy of a voice creates an intimacy between storyteller and listener that may or may not be present in a book of prose. It has been our utmost concern to maintain the integrity of Andy's voice while editing the commentaries for print. When in doubt about the necessity of a change, we've erred on the side of letting things be.

Thus, in matters of mechanical style, we decided to go with what seemed to us the most reader-friendly prose. The names of birds and plants are styled lowercase, as they would be in the vernacular. We believe this presents a collection that is most approachable for a wide readership. We hope that ornithologists and other specialists see the usefulness of such a decision.

If you've been a listener of his commentary, you know that there is something about the way Andy engages with nature. Andy doesn't notice a lizard—he has a showdown with it. He writes with admirable self-deprecation about a close encounter with an alligator. For twenty years, he has openly and without apology shared his love for the natural world in three- and four-minute clips on the air. And now he shares some of his wistful moments culled from that time on the page.

If you haven't yet listened to Andy's commentary, no matter. As Andy himself said at the conception of the book, "I want people of all ages to want to get up and go mess around outside after reading my book." Read for educational purposes, read to relax and envision the world, but most of all, read and then get ready to literally get your hands dirty and your feet wet. For if Andy has accomplished his goal, you'll want to discover the abundance that still exists around us every day, in our back yards of Carolina.

LOUISA JONAS, Editor

Since 1992, Andy has been involved in the study and propagation of rare freshwater snails endemic only to southeastern North Carolina. A portion of the proceeds from the sale of Backyard Carolina *will help fund ongoing projects to protect two species of these endangered snails.*

BACKYARD CAROLINA
TWO DECADES OF
PUBLIC RADIO COMMENTARY

1

In the Back Yard

Morning Singsong

MARCH 2001 The morning sky was cloudy, and rain was in the forecast—a welcome thought, considering the short supply we have enjoyed so far this year. It was 6:35 a.m. I was watching the horizon brighten off to the east when, all of a sudden, I heard the song of an amorous northern cardinal, heralding the blossoming day. The cardinal was calling from underneath a large wax myrtle shrub growing where my vegetable garden once was. It's still a garden, technically, only it no longer supports typical vegetable garden fare like tomatoes and cucumbers; rather, it's now a place for various wildflowers and other fallow plants, including the trio of stately myrtles that serve as shelters for singing cardinals and other songbirds.

The cardinal was a bit of a surprise. Before it, mornings were dutifully heralded by a pair of Carolina wrens that also live in our yard. Back in February the wrens would begin their morning soliloquy well before six in the morning, waking even the crows, who would add their calls a few minutes after the wrens started. The cardinals at that time were very subdued in their vocalizing and audible only when they joined with other birds to scold some passing hawk.

3

The day our backyard cardinal started the morning singsong was significant because it meant something was changing in the yard. That change had very much to do with spring and avian courtship. The cardinal was beginning a new level of bonding with his mate, whom I looked for from my vantage point on the back porch, but she was playing coy and not moving. He, on the other hand, stood out red and bold, flap-hopping from branchtip to branchtip, pausing only long enough to emit a series of smooth whistles and chirrups.

I thought it curious that the wrens were silent during the cardinal's initial performance, and I began to wonder if there was a communal understanding among the backyard birds that required some to be silent when others were courting. Then, suddenly, the wren spoke up, bolting out a high-pitched, lilting piece that was rather cardinal-like, save for its higher key and tempo. So much for courtesy.

The male cardinal kept up his singing in spite of the wren's apparent efforts to upstage him, and as I listened to the competing soloists, I finally caught sight of the orange-brown female cardinal, perched on a dense patch of myrtle leaves just a few feet from the male. It was soon obvious the two were a pair; as he called, she slowly drew closer to him, and at her approach his calls changed to a series of delicate, whistle-like cheeps.

The change in his song made it easier to hear the song of the blue jay out in the front yard. At first I'd thought the jay was scolding something, maybe a passing cat or hawk. This theory was bolstered by the sounds of a few more blue jays joining in. I went around front to see what the group had spied and found five blue jays cavorting in the uppermost branches of our yard's tallest sycamore tree. They were

4

scrambling about, some thirty feet overhead, loudly singing their *queedle, queedle* song, interspersed with an occasional imitation of a hawk's call. I stayed in the front yard to watch. The birds were focused on each other, not some threatening interloper. They performed a casual, springy, flap-hopping dance similar to the male cardinal's display in the backyard shrubbery; this behavior seemed like a shared sort of courtship display. As the jays' dancing continued, the tones of their voices lowered to quiet murmurs, again reminding me of the cardinal's behavior. Then one of the birds flew off without so much as a by-your-leave. The movements of the other birds quieted to a stop, and as quickly as they'd gathered, the remaining jays departed toward the back yard, not as individuals, but two at a time, each pair looking and behaving for all the world like the bonded couples they had become.

A Near Miss

APRIL 2001 Last weekend I was given the task of removing a tangle of landscape plants that had overgrown their bounds in my mother-in-law's yard. I made a rather sobering discovery in the process.

With loppers and hand pruners at the ready, I proceeded to undo years of ignored growth on a particularly large euonymus shrub, an evergreen landscape plant that suffers from molds and mildews and one that also shows signs of being somewhat invasive. Straight and lanky from the low-light conditions, the plant's stems were easy to cut near their bases.

Once under way, I worked at a pretty feverish pace. I cut a branch here, a stem there, and pulled out one after another, reveling in the good work I was accomplishing—and then I saw it. Tucked into the crotch of one of the branches I was on the verge of cutting was a bird's nest. I immediately felt a pang of guilt for what I had done. I quickly realized that the frantic chirps I heard from a nearby cardinal were the worryings of the female I had unknowingly frightened off her nest.

A search of the ground under and around the nest site revealed no spilt eggs or young birds. The discovery of the nest, however, made me aware how reckless I had been. I'd known that it was bird-nesting season, and that birds, including cardinals, mockingbirds, and Carolina wrens, had each, at one time or another, chosen this particular yard as a site to raise their young. Needless to say, I quit my assault upon the euonymus bush, and the female cardinal returned to her nest.

As I collected the debris from my efforts, the tragedy of what could have happened really sank in. The nest was actively occupied, with parent birds incubating a clutch of eggs that promised to soon become a hungry brood of nestlings. I felt relieved—but only a little—because dumb luck was the only thing that spared these birds' home. I should have taken care to check the branches for nests before beginning my task.

Some may feel I'm taking this situation too seriously, especially because the nest remained undamaged. But I belabor it because this experience serves as stark testimony for what's happening all over our community right now on a much larger scale. Instead of hand pruners clipping a branch here and there, there are bulldozers pushing down trees and crushing entire woodlands for the sake of buildings and lots. The wholesale destruction of trees and woods is tragic enough, considering how precious these resources are in a community rapidly dominated by cement, clay, and glass. And when you add in the loss of songbirds, turtles, and butterflies, the tragedy becomes monumental.

By now I suspect some folks are wondering just how out of touch I am with reality. After all, they're just trees; do I expect us to stifle growth and development for some trees, butterflies, and birds? Maybe a little. I worry that our children will look back on our current habitat-destroying behavior and scorn us for despoiling their own children's natural heritage. We're now going through this same cycle, wishing our forebears hadn't brought about the extinction of the Carolina parakeet, the ivory-billed woodpecker, and the passenger pigeon.

I realize there's a difference between the near destruction of a single cardinal nest and the extinction of an entire species. But the thought of extinction never entered the minds of bygone hunters and loggers when passenger pigeons darkened their skies in tremendous flocks. These birds just disappeared, along with the aforementioned woodpecker and parakeet, mostly due to habitat loss. Loss of habitat is the greatest threat today's cardinals face. I can try to be mindful of birds' nests when I clip and prune shrubs. I just wish bulldozers could do the same.

A Lizard's Indignation

JUNE 1999 During a particularly harsh spell of hot, dry weather, I decided to make rounds in my yard to water some of my thirstier potted plants. While I was focused on finding the plants in greatest need, the cool water from the hose disturbed a retiring Carolina anole lizard that had been using one of the plants as a rest area. The lizard jumped briskly out of the water's path and paused for a moment on a large cedar stump left in the yard as a memorial to Hurricane Fran, which blew down the tree three years earlier.

The stump is now a favorite sunning spot for several lizards that call our yard their home. This one's bright green body caught my attention, and even though the anole is a common beast around here, I ceased my watering activity so I could admire him. When I shut off the water, the lizard cocked his head to make eye contact with me. He then proceeded to lift the forward part of his torso off the stump, as if doing a push-up, and he extended a folded flap of skin on his throat. This throat fan, also called a dewlap, was a lovely (or should I say handsome) color, a mix of salmon-pink with a hint of lavender in it.

The lizard's throat fan was about the size of a thumbnail, stretching along the midline of his neck almost to his front

Carolina anole, *Anolis carolinensis*

limbs. As soon as the dewlap was extended, the lizard followed through with his push-up stance by quickly bobbing his head and chest up and down, using the stump as a workout platform. The lizard's motions were meant to draw attention to himself; they're especially helpful when trying to attract the attention of a nearby female. Anoles also employ similar motions when rival males trespass into one another's territory, although I have to admit that the subtle nuances that distinguish courtship display from threat display are lost on me.

At the time of our encounter I was wearing a bleached-white shirt, so I doubt the anole thought I was another lizard. His body language most likely spoke volumes of lizard expletives reserved typically for predators a lizard is confident it can outrun. I looked the lizard over and saw that he bore several small black marks on his body, along with a hairline crack in an otherwise immaculate tail. The black scars and the near fracture told of past battles with other lizards, or possibly some kind of predator—regardless, it was clear that this lizard was a survivor and a force to reckon with.

We continued to eye each other for another minute, the lizard and I, and as I watched him I felt a pang of guilt, owing to his seeming indignation regarding my watering accident. I wondered if I had truly offended this lizard's pride. Were his animated dewlap threats a veiled attempt at restoring some semblance of dignity? At the risk of sounding anthropomorphic, I decided I'd have to answer yes to both counts.

Yucca Bug!

JUNE 1989 When the soft-leaved yucca plant in my front yard recently sent up two tall stalks that resembled oversized asparagus, I eagerly anticipated the flowery show I knew they would soon produce. I also looked forward to a visit from an old acquaintance I knew from Texas: the pastel-white yucca moth.

Waiting patiently as the days rolled by, I watched the flower stalk sprout small fingerlike buds that soon opened into creamy white flowers like papery bells waving in the breeze.

Yucca moths visit yucca plants soon after the plant sends up its flower stalk. The female yucca moth pollinates the yucca flower just after laying her eggs in the flower ovary. This delicate insect's eggs hatch into quarter-inch-long caterpillars that are colored a pale whitish green like that of the yucca plant's seed pods. The caterpillars eat the soft, fruity part of the yucca seeds, but the plant produces an ample amount, and many of the seeds survive the caterpillar onslaught.

But instead of attracting my hoped-for moths, these flowers actually drew another interesting insect, this one known as the leaf-footed bug. And my yucca plant drew a lot of them. On one stalk alone I counted over fifty individuals; this wasn't an easy tally, because as I counted, they continuously changed position on the plant. These particular leaf-footed bugs were chocolate-brown overall, with a slender yellow band running across their backs. They're called leaf-footed because their hindmost legs are much larger than their foremost, sporting a serrated, flattened, leaflike feature at the ends, the function of which is open to debate. The yucca moth and the leaf-footed bug are both insects, but the leaf-footed bug is a true bug. This may seem a trivial point, and to most people it is. But to someone who enjoys calling another creature by its appropriate name, this distinction is worth mention.

Applied correctly, the term "bug" refers to an elite group of insects known as the Hemiptera—a scientific name that means "half-wing," because their first pair of leathery wings cover only half of their abdomens. I know this is a small point. All true bugs have a piercing-sucking mouthpart, and newly hatched young bugs resemble their adult form. Development in other insects includes a larva stage and pupa stage, neither of which remotely resembles the finished adult form. For example, a yucca moth is first an egg, then a larva (called a caterpillar), then a pupa, and finally an adult moth.

Just as all dogs are mammals, and not all mammals are dogs, it's also true that all bugs are insects, but not all insects are bugs. This isn't really an important enough issue to become a pet peeve, but a lot of non-bugs are wrongly called bugs. Take one of the stars of nursery rhymes, for example: the ladybird beetle. These orange-and-black insects are beetles, not bugs—but how often do we hear them called ladybugs?

Or how about water bugs? What I think of when I hear the name water bug is a large one- to two-inch-long aquatic true bug with curved, scimitar-like front legs used to capture prey. You can understand my confusion when I first heard someone say their house was being invaded by water bugs. What they were referring to, of course, was a large species of cockroach, and not the true predatory (and beneficial) water bug. Interestingly enough, the reviled cockroach is more closely related to the praying mantis than to any true bug.

Or how about the roly-poly that children adore so much? These armored leaf-litter inhabitants are also called sow bugs or pill bugs, but they're actually crustaceans, more closely related to crabs and barnacles than to bugs, or any insect for that matter.

The name *bug* seems to be applied most frequently to creepy-crawly things in the house, including spiders. This too is an incorrect use of the name. Spiders are eight-legged arachnids with two body parts: a fused head and thorax, called a cephalothorax, and the larger body part called the abdomen. Insects are six-legged creatures with three body parts, including a distinct head, thorax, and abdomen.

My list of misnamed animals is lengthy, and I won't cover them all in one sitting, but it certainly includes other creatures besides insects. Minnows, for instance, are not merely baby fish. The name *minnow* refers to the family Cyprinidae of fish, which includes goldfish and other carps, some exceeding five feet in length.

Just as a rose is a rose, so too is a bug a bug. My point is: the more we know about an animal, whether it's an insect, a fish, or a snake, the greater chance we'll have of coexisting with it. And I believe there is no better place to begin that happy coexistence than by addressing something by its proper name.

So the next time you see a "bug" crawling across your floor or patio, look closely to be sure of what it is. I think if you take the time to do this, you might find less inclination to stomp it.

Garden Friends

JULY 2003 I was outside watering some potted plants when I suddenly found myself the attention of a pair of rather large flying insects called digger wasps. These wasps are named after the female's habit of digging nest chambers in the ground, into which she stuffs immobilized crickets and grasshoppers that will later serve as food for her developing larvae. The digger wasps in my longleaf-pine yard are close to an inch long and about as big around as a pencil. They are pale brown in color, with even paler yellowish rings around their abdomen. Their large wings, which make a rather deep, humming sound, are cola-colored, and heavily veined for structural support.

This is a busy time of year for the inquisitive digger wasps; they can often be seen flying low to the ground, investigating every plant leaf and stem growing less than a few feet off the ground, in hopes of spying an unwary cricket or grasshopper. When I stepped into their territory, they must have mistaken me for a new plant to explore, because two of them flew up and, in a methodical, hovering manner, scoured me from the waist down. Digger wasps are inoffensive creatures for the most part—sure, the females will sting if provoked, but they really have no reason to sting anything bigger than a cricket, as that would be a waste of energy and venom. Almost as a rule, you can expect the solitary wasps, which include the diggers, sand wasps, thread-waists, spider-hunters, and ichneumon wasps, to be disinclined to sting us humans (again, unless provoked). Their colony-dwelling relatives, the paper wasps, are another matter entirely.

It was while I was watching the digger wasps investigating me that I chanced to see another large and somewhat imposing-looking beast fly into view. It was a wasp mimic, meant to resemble a big, black-and-orange spider-hunting wasp. It had me fooled for a moment, but one look at its short, straight antennae and very flylike pair of eyes, and I was positive that it was none other than the mydas fly, an uncommon, heavy-legged relative of the robber fly. And like the robber fly, the mydas preys on other flying insects, including big horseflies and even some bees.

Mydas flies are large-bodied black insects with an orange band around the base of their abdomen, near where it joins the insect's midsection. The color band is kind of hard to see, unless they're in flight. The same general description holds true for this fly's model, the solitary spider wasp, except that the wasp has curled antennae and a bluish iridescent shine to its wings and abdomen. Mydas fly wings are flat black and the abdomen is somewhat furry, lacking the wasp's shine.

The fly landed on a log not far from where one of the digger wasps was excavating a nest chamber. Mydas flies have keen eyesight, so to sneak up on it I had to use both of my hands—I kept its attention on one hand, which I held in front of it, slightly wiggling my fingers as I did so, while slowly encroaching on it from behind with my other hand. The ruse worked, but as I tried to pin the fly down, it used its stout, claw-tipped legs to extricate itself and wing a short distance to another landing site.

The fly was a quick learner, and my second attempt at its capture ended before I even got within two feet of it, so I resigned myself to just watching it work the yard, chasing horseflies and deerflies.

If you spend time outdoors on a midsummer weekend, keep your eyes open for mydas flies and other unusual flying insects. And keep in mind that many large flying insects are our allies in the yard, feeding on other insects that might otherwise bite us or our garden plants.

Of Wasps and Bees

AUGUST 1997 I was sitting out on the back porch with some friends the other day when I found myself becoming increasingly engrossed in the persistent flybys of a pair of brightly colored yellow jackets. I wasn't concerned that they would sting us; I was just curious to know what they were looking around for.

Yellow jackets are members of the wasp group of insects, a large membership that also includes ants and bees. I've always had great respect for yellow jackets because they pack a potent sting delivered by a hair-thin stinger resembling a tiny hypodermic needle. It works equally well as a defensive weapon as it does an offensive food-gathering device, at least for females of the group. Male bees and wasps (and their relatives, the ants) lack stingers, as the stinger is actually a modified egg-laying device.

Wasp stingers differ from bee stingers—bees have tiny barbs on their stingers, whereas wasp stingers are smooth and barb-free. This difference is significant. When a bee stings, the stinger holds fast in the flesh of its victim, and when the bee flies off, the bee's venom gland and its surrounding muscles get ripped from its body, with fatal consequences for the bee. This is why bees are generally reluctant to sting. And it's not nice for the victim either, because the muscle around the bee's venom gland will continue to push venom through the stinger. Wasps, on the other hand, can sting as much as they like, because their stinger is designed to aid in food gathering first and defense second. While both solitary and colonial wasps can survive the attack, colonial wasps are generally more aggressive and may be quick to sting to defend a hive.

I don't always ponder this difference when I see a yellow jacket, but this particular encounter had me wondering if other potential sting victims, such as spiders, gave it any thought. Next to where I was sitting was a perfect little spider web, about as big around as a small dinner plate. It was a type called an orb web, due to its symmetrical round shape. The spider itself was nowhere to be seen but I was sure it was nearby, because its web, like the plate whose size it resembled, held a collection of recently captured insect meals. There were six of them all together, each tightly trussed up and suspended in a vertical line right down the middle of the web. Each package was about the size of a grain of wild rice, and about the same color.

I watched the two yellow jackets make their way along the porch rail, flying in a back-and-forth manner. When they came upon the spider web, one of the little packets suddenly dropped from the center of the lattice-like orb and stayed motionless beneath it, attached to the end of a nearly invisible strand of silk. I was surprised to see that this was the very spider that had made the web, and that I'd mistaken it for one of the six little packets I saw lined up in a row. It was cleverly disguised as one of its suspended meals, and had the yellow jackets not come upon it I would never have known it was there. Yellow jackets and certain species of other wasps are capable of capturing a spider right out of the web. Somehow aware of the threat posed by the yellow jackets, this plucky little spider ducked away from harm before the yellow jackets noticed it. Having seen no spider around the web, the yellow jackets flew off in search of other prey, and soon after, the little spider climbed back into its position in the web. I was curious to know what tipped off the spider to the potential threat of the winged predators; I assumed it must have been a visual cue, so I wiggled my finger at the spider to try to coax it to drop, but whatever visual threat I thought I was simulating had no apparent effect on the spider, as it just sat in its web and ignored me.

I'm still not sure what triggered the spider to flee its web at the yellow jackets' approach. Maybe it was the rush of wind generated by the yellow jackets' wings, or maybe one of the yellow jackets inadvertently touched the web and I just hadn't seen it happen. But what really made me curious about the spider's ability to discern one flying insect from another was that, among the spider's catches, there were no fewer than three small sweat bees. These small insects are so named because they often land on perspiring skin, evidently in search of salt. Sweat bees can sting, but they don't hunt spiders; this little spider was somehow able to figure that out in time to turn the bees into a meal. Just one more example of a spider's curious abilities, made clear right in one's own back yard.

Mowing for Crickets

SEPTEMBER 1995 Summer must be drawing to a close, because this week I went out and mowed my yard. When I was a kid, yard mowing was simply a task to get through. It provided little in the way of entertainment, but it did allow me a small income—or actually two kinds of small incomes. There were cash dollars and cash animals, and I welcomed both. The cash dollar income enabled me to buy terrariums and gear to house my growing collection of snakes, turtles, and frogs.

The other income came in the form of crickets and grasshoppers, and this currency was often more valuable than cash dollars, because back then, I didn't know of any places to buy crickets to feed my frogs and toads. I had to collect their food by hand, and this effort was aided in large part by my lawn mower, which scared crickets out of hiding every time.

I'm now lucky enough to have a Saint Augustine–grass yard to shape into something other than a monotonous lawn. Plus I have the added benefit of being able to catch crickets in my own yard. Even though today I could go out and buy a batch of crickets to feed my animals, I still prefer yard-raised crickets over the store-bought kind, much the same way some people prefer farmyard chicken eggs over supermarket eggs. I believe yard-raised crickets are a little tougher than the store brands—just their look and feel says vitamin-rich, super-nutritious food packets. My lawn-mowing efforts are frequently interrupted by the visage of a jumping cricket, which I'll immediately pursue. Each one serves as an interesting distraction to an otherwise mundane task, so I've developed a habit of mowing circles around potentially valuable tree seedlings and unknown wildflowers, to better my chances at finding crickets.

In addition to the bounty of yard crickets my mowing yields, my late-summer tradition provides me with a chance to assess my yard's overall condition. Like most yards, mine is dominated by grass, but it's not just Saint Augustine turf-grass. There's also a healthy stand of my favorite bunch-grass, known as the little bluestem, which, true to its name, sports a flush of new, vibrant blue-green leaf growth in early summer. And as autumn ensues, the blue-green will change to shades of blond and amber yellow. My habit of mowing around such pioneer grasses has, over several years, created a miniature bluestem grass meadow that now encompasses about one-fifth of the front yard area.

This bluestem meadow is home to several Carolina anole lizards that I often see cavorting about—especially the males, who spar with one another by extending their lavender-colored throat fans and vigorously bobbing their heads. I occasionally spot a broadhead skink basking on the big piece of driftwood I placed amid the tall grasses. Broad-head skinks are heavy, smooth-scaled, shiny lizards that can grow to over ten inches long. Male broadheads have a nearly triangular-shaped head that turns a vivid, brassy orange in contrast to their otherwise chocolate-brown body during spring breeding season. The broadhead in my front yard can really strike an impressive dragonlike pose when he sprawls out on the driftwood. The much smaller anoles—normally bold and aggressive among their own kind—never seem quite so confident of themselves when the big broadhead is around.

In late summer, when crickets are at their peak in the turf and the tall goldenrod flowers are setting their yellow blooms, my yard is visited by monarch butterflies working their way south toward Mexico for the winter. The goldenrod also attracts lemon-yellow sulfur butterflies, along with huge tiger swallowtails and my autumn butterfly favorite, the long-tailed skipper. All of these late-summer treasures visit or stay in my yard because of the diverse array of plants that grow on their own, with no help from me other than my mowing the turfgrass back down once in a while.

I knew my efforts at creating a front-yard wildlife habitat were really paying off when I saw small sapling trees sticking up from the little islands of tall grass and wildflowers. These islands were originally created by consistently mowing a circle around a clump of grass or seedling tree. Soon each island grew into its own microhabitat, some harboring an oak or a cedar, a wax myrtle or a yaupon, or a patch of bluestem grasses and goldenrod. In another yard, these little anchor plants may have been seen as little more than weeds—plants audaciously growing in a place where someone believes they shouldn't be.

I'm proud of my front-yard habitat because it started humbly, as two clumps of volunteer bluestem grass, and has since grown into a dense wooded grove of red cedar and water oaks. The shade from the small trees forced the bluestems and goldenrods to the outer edges, where the butterflies could still access them. With my passive management style, the only "weed" I have to contend with now is the Saint Augustine turf.

Over the years that I've nurtured our not-so-turf yard, I remind myself of the reason I mow the way I do: it's fun to watch what happens and see who moves in when you simply let things go a little wild. This week, having contemplated that, I decided to dump my jar of jumping crickets and watch them disappear into the safety of the yard.

The Surprise of Fran

SEPTEMBER 1996 Like so many other people's yards in southeastern North Carolina, mine was not spared the ravages of Hurricane Fran. But for all the losses my yard and its inhabitants suffered, I can already see renewals and recoveries.

My family and I were very fortunate regarding Fran's timing: the surge of tidal waters created by the storm stopped no more than one-eighth of an inch from entering our house. The garden tiller, lawn mower, water pump, and other various things in the yard were less fortunate, but, having gone through two major floods in Texas years earlier, I can say we were lucky.

I stayed at home with my family for the duration of the storm, watching as the wind stripped leaves from the sycamore trees out front and pushed down two massive cedars, one at each end of the house. And we watched the water rise from Bradley Creek—salty water, straight from the ocean. The rising water carried every form of bottle, jar, plastic, foam, and other buoyant matter that had been at rest somewhere in the expanse of marsh behind our house. Boards, grasses, sticks, and branches all found their way into our yard.

And while this debris was a chore to collect, pile, and compost, it's the water that wreaked true havoc on my yard. In the years we had lived on Bradley Creek, we had put considerable effort into creating a yard both for wildlife and for us. I care quite a lot about the frogs and newts and snails and birds living in my yard, because I consider them part of my extended family. But as I watched the water rise with Hurricane Fran, I was too concerned for my immediate family to realize I was losing some dear friends.

The salty water flooded above-ground ponds and tanks, buckets and barrels, aquariums, terrariums, and every inch of backyard habitat my family and I had put together over the years. The magnitude of the event sank in just as the water ceased rising and I knew the worst of the storm was over. By flashlight I could see that three years' work of propagating an obscure and very rare freshwater snail had just been dealt a setback that would further jeopardize the species' hopes for survival.

I discovered that three generations of broken-striped newts were lost to the briny water. Gone too were thousands of twenty-one-day-old green frog tadpoles, and, I assumed, their parents. My good friends the adult bullfrogs, I could only hope, had been pushed onto higher ground somewhere up stream.

Just before Fran's eye passed over, I waded into the rising flood—a foolhardy effort now that I look back on it, and one that put my wife, Sandy, and our two young boys on edge. For the risk, I was able to rescue only twelve individual snails from one of the plastic ponds just as it was being heaved over by the flood. As luck would have it, I had a small aquarium with clean rainwater in the house where I was able to harbor the lucky dozen.

I spent most of the early morning hours waiting for the winds to fall so I could begin to search the yard. With daylight I realized the snails were my greatest loss. Five pools flooded, the salty torrent washing away hundreds of individual snails from the class of '96, dozens from '95, and a handful from '94. But just as despair was setting in, a few really neat things happened. Sandy found a female spotted turtle hunkered in the roots of an uprooted pecan tree. She was one of my road rescues who shared a breeding pen with three other spotteds, along with some box turtles.

Soon after the spotted turtle find, I heard our younger son, Carson, discover a box turtle. Suddenly a search for the missing became a discovery of how much life was still around: a five-lined skink, then a glass lizard (more properly called a legless lizard, owing to its natural limbless look). Then another spotted turtle, discovered by our older son, Robin; two young bull froglets, just transformed from tadpoles; swallowtail butterflies flitting haphazardly about; and of all things, a lovely male bluebird!

Most amazing of all was a discovery in one of the outdoor aquariums that had been submerged under the floodwater. I resigned myself that the yearling spotted turtle and yellow-bellied pond turtle that had been living in that tank were long gone, but at Robin and Carson's insistence I groped around in the murky water, and to our collective delight they were both still there. How they managed to stay put during the flood, I will never know.

Finding these two little turtles was like being reunited with lost loved ones. And that's how it continued in the days after the storm: a box turtle hatchling found under a pile of dead cordgrass; another spotted turtle, this one wallowing in the shallows of one of the snail pools. We even found a not-so-bedraggled leopard frog sitting amid some tattered, though living, pickerelweed growing in a five-gallon bucket.

And as though they knew we needed the lift, house wrens, thrashers, cardinals, and blue jays all appeared in the storm-wracked shrubs and trees. They were all coming back, and will continue to do so after every storm, I hope, just like the rest of us.

A Saddleback's Sting

OCTOBER 2001 My family and I were engaged in some autumn yard cleaning recently when both my wife and my younger son had the misfortune of brushing into one of our area's most painful stinging little insects. Sandy was the first to encounter this cryptic creature while we were clipping some wax myrtle shrubs. She was reaching into some branches and suddenly she felt a searing pain on her arm. There were no welts where the pain was—which would've been a telltale sign of a wasp sting—but there was a rashlike mark. Thinking about it for a moment, I concluded that the most likely culprit was an uncommon insect called the saddleback caterpillar, one of the few insects that choose to eat the aromatic leaves of the wax myrtle shrub. A quick search of the plant confirmed my theory.

Now, before you decide to run out and chop down your wax myrtle shrubs or blanket your yard with broad-spectrum pesticide, let me explain a little about the saddleback caterpillar.

Saddlebacks are also called slug caterpillars, because they creep along plant branches and leaves in a very sluglike fashion. In spite of this similarity, saddleback caterpillars, unlike some slugs, are actually quite attractive. They're less than an inch long and about the diameter of a pencil. Their middle section is a delightful shade of lime green, broken by an oval-shaped purple or brown saddle patch—hence the caterpillar's common name. The caterpillar's front and rear ends are rich brown, and each end sports raised protuberances bristling with short, hollow spines. The front region contains one prominent pair of spiny growths, with two more pairs of smaller spine clusters that wrap over and protect the caterpillar's head.

The caterpillar's rear end contains the same kind of spine clusters, with an additional feature: a pair of bright yellow false eye spots just behind the larger pair of spine clusters. False eye spots are common features of many kinds of animals and are believed to confuse or frighten predators; but in the case of the saddleback, any predator going after it from either direction will be in for a painful surprise. Filling out the caterpillar's armament is a pair of lateral lines running along each side. The lines are punctuated by seven tiny clusters of spines, making the caterpillar's overall appearance, when viewed through a lens, strangely reminiscent of a small, furry dog. Or maybe I've been looking at them too long.

The saddleback's business ends are its spines. They contain a powerful toxin rivaling that of any small wasp or bee; caterpillar-hunting wasps are about the only predators that can penetrate the saddleback's defensive shield. Caterpillars are not offensive creatures, however, and injuries to people are usually the result of inadvertently touching the animal.

In the event that a saddleback caterpillar is encountered, all the victim can do is try to remove any embedded spines—sticky tape helps with that. Apply rubbing alcohol to help denature the toxin, apply cold compresses, and if serious reactions occur, seek medical attention immediately.

Sandy's injury abated within fifteen minutes, most likely because she merely brushed against the animal. Carson, on the other hand, was less fortunate. His injury came while collecting clipped branches and was made worse by his actually grabbing the animal, which drove the spines deep into the skin of his middle finger. There was surprisingly little swelling or redness to show where the injury was located, but the pain took almost an hour to start quieting down.

We typically find saddleback caterpillars in autumn because this is when they become full-grown larvae. In the coming weeks they spin cocoons to overwinter in, and they complete their metamorphosis and emerge from their cocoons as small, dark brown moths. After mating, the female moth will lay her eggs on a number of different kinds of trees and shrubs, including the wax myrtle, and the larvae will begin their lives by feasting on the shrubs beneath them.

As potentially painful as an encounter with one of these creatures may be, it's important to note that saddlebacks are not a very common presence in typical landscapes, and trying to eradicate them chemically or otherwise would inevitably result in doing harm to plenty of other, non-target species, including natural predators that may actually be helping to hold the saddleback in check.

We may never understand the role this strange creature plays in the environment, but as with many other local denizens, the saddleback caterpillar is one thread in the tapestry of life in our back yards.

Where Have All the Songbirds Gone?

NOVEMBER 1994 It seems that for the past few years, at about this time, more and more people ask me the same disturbing question: Why aren't the birds coming to the feeders?

I wish I could give a simple answer—something like, "Maybe they aren't all that hungry," or, "They just haven't migrated into our area yet." And it could just be that the shortage of songbirds at our feeding stations is indicative of an overall decline in North American songbird populations. But the truth is, I can't provide a simple, one-line explanation for the apparent shortage of songbirds. I'm not sure if anyone can.

I believe the lack of birds around the house is due to a combination of factors. North American songbird populations over the past twenty years have slipped consistently downward; even familiar songbirds like the blue jay and the robin are declining, mostly because so many of their habitats have been lost. Other less familiar songbirds—buntings and warblers, for example—are also in trouble because of habitat loss, especially in our region, which serves as summer breeding ground for many songbird species.

This habitat loss is profound enough to be a continent-wide threat. Natural habitats provide four key elements for the survival of birds (and other wildlife): food, water, shelter, and a place to live. Agriculture, housing, and suburban sprawl combine to produce an alien landscape that's inhospitable to the kinds of animals adapted to a woodland lifestyle. So putting out bird feeders in winter may be helpful, but it's not enough: in addition to food and water, the birds need shelter and space to live and raise their young.

I also attribute the perceived absence of songbirds to the time of year; it's now late fall, and there is an abundance of wild fruits and berries hanging from just about every bush, shrub, tree, and vine in our area. This year's good crop of wild fruits is providing a much needed respite for birds and other fruit-eaters whose food supplies are reduced by habitat loss. The songbirds we expect to see at our feeders are probably around—they just aren't around our feeders yet.

Songbirds depend on habitats every moment of every day. Their continued existence requires constant exercise. They work to find food and water, and to build a nest to shelter their eggs and young, and they must work to defend their territory from rival birds and predators.

Over the past several years, in a small attempt to counter habitat loss, I've let nature run somewhat free in my yard. My once-manicured lawn has become a managed ecological landscape suitable for songbirds and other local denizens. The adventures this shift in outlook has provided me have been unbounded, from discovering little clumps of inconspicuous mosses and ferns to observing a Cooper's hawk attack cardinals at the seed station. This latter example is the measuring stick I use to determine the ultimate success of a bird-feeding station. The seed attracts the songbirds, and if the songbirds are numerous they'll attract the Cooper's hawks—though this year, such dramas have not begun at my feeders, or at least not yet.

If we compare the numbers of birds we saw at feeders in 1994 to those seen in 1974, we'd clearly realize that the numbers we remember attracting in years past cannot be repeated, regardless of how much seed we put out. That alone is reason to redouble our efforts to prevent habitat loss by creating backyard wildlife habitats. I suggest you start by letting nature take over just ten percent of your yard. You can let her have more as you learn to appreciate the reduced workload and the wonders that come with a habitat yard. In the meantime, with winter approaching, keep the feeders stocked with fresh seed, and resolve to take a course of action that will convert your yard into a habitat haven. That way our backyard birds—and we in turn—will have less to despair, and more to celebrate.

Thanksgiving Mole

NOVEMBER 2002 Thanksgiving is a time when many Americans think about food. I've discovered a seldom-seen resident that thinks of little else year round.

While I don't expect to see many people in our area plowing through the soil in search of tasty treats, I do expect to see at least one of our local creatures doing as much. Or at least I'll see its effect on the ground: a meandering ridge of soil snaking across the landscape. These ridges are the trademarks of the mole, an interesting member of a specialized group of mammals called insectivores, a family that also includes the tiny, mouselike shrews.

Moles are not related to mice, other than the fact that both are mammals. Mice are rodents with large, chisel-like incisor teeth, designed for gnawing hard seeds. Moles, on the other hand, are fierce predators with pointed teeth, including needle-sharp canines that serve to grab small subterranean insects and worms. Moles are covered with the softest coat of hairs I have ever felt, and they are very warm to the touch because they lose heat energy rapidly, owing to their high metabolic rate. Their almost velvety coat helps to keep soil from clinging to them as they tunnel about, and their small eyes and ears are designed to have less surface area for particles of dirt to get into (plus, in a dark tunnel, who needs good eyesight?).

Moles tunnel through moist sand or loamy soil by pushing their conical head forward and then sweeping the material aside with their broad, spade-shaped front limbs. It looks like a difficult task, and it can be, where soils are dense or where plant roots form thick mats. In the right conditions a healthy mole can excavate ten to fifteen yards of tunnels in one hour, which makes it difficult to track one down in its lair. The ridges on the surface of the ground are actually hunting routes. The sleeping and nest quarters of the mole lie a foot or more deep, and often under a log or other similar structure. Moles line their nests with bits of dried grass and leaves, and in the spring, these insulated places provide safety to the mole's brood of two to four offspring. Most moles are solitary creatures that interact with each other only during the courtship and mating season.

We have a resident mole near our house right now that has established a network of surface tunnels along the edge of our driveway and, in places, under it. The soil is almost pure sand and the driveway is little more than a thin layer of gravel, and each morning you can see where the mole has traveled, including the places in its hunting trail that it repaired after a careless foot or car tire caved it in. The tunneling being done in my yard, however, isn't a problem for me or anything growing there, save for the odd earthworm, beetle grub, or other sumptuous delicacy the mole chooses to eat.

And eating is what moles are all about. They have an almost insatiable appetite due to their high metabolism— a typical mole weighs only about as much as a chicken's egg, but will consume its own weight in food every day. If deprived of worms or insects for even a few hours, a mole will wane like a battery losing its charge, only to suddenly go dead of starvation.

Many lawn owners detest the idea of moles burrowing through their yards, but the moles burrow only to get food, including underground Japanese beetle larvae, which as adults survive by chewing on various landscape plant leaves and flowers. So moles should really be seen as beneficial insect controllers and soil aerators, rather than unwelcome guests in our yards. They may create unsightly messes as they eat, but then, at Thanksgiving, who doesn't? Maybe this Thanksgiving, the moles can be forgiven and allowed to dine quietly on appetizers of plump beetle grubs, followed by a hearty course of earthworms. Hmm, just the thought of it makes me thankful I'm not a mole—please pass me that bowl of . . . what did you say those were?

Green Lynx

DECEMBER 2004 Back in October I found a lovely green spider nestled amid the blooms of a bright orange milkweed plant growing alongside my driveway. The spider was easy to find because it had wrapped a clump of milkweed flowers in a loose tangle of spider silk that made the flowers look like a small wad of cotton candy. The telltale webbing is a giveaway once you know what you're looking at, and before long I spied the sharp-eyed female relaxed within her silken parlor.

I recognized the spider as a member of the lynx spider clan, and a female, judging from its nearly three-quarter-inch-long body (the male lynx spider is at best a quarter-inch long).

Lynx spiders make for easy study, because they stay in the same clump of grass or flowers once they've settled down and are ready to raise a family. Female lynx spiders are doting and protective mothers, and the individual I found in the milkweed was no exception. Within a week of finding her, I saw a silken globe about a half-inch across that was secured to one of the flower stems. The globe of course was an egg case, within which, I presume, resided some hundred-odd eggs that the green lynx diligently stood vigil over. I checked on her nearly every day for the remainder of October and through the first half of November, and each visit found her on duty in a leggy embrace of her cherished egg case.

In early November the eggs hatched, and for the first few days the newly hatched spiders, tiny replicas of their mother, clung tight to their egg case. However, the eighth-inch-long spiderlings soon began to venture a couple inches afield, maybe driven by hunger, while their mother watched them with her shiny eight eyes. The volume of tiny spiders may have been a nightmarish vision to an arachnophobe, but the little beasts were no threat to anything larger than them, and actually, they're the ones they need watch out for, because a young lynx spider's first meal may indeed be a brother or sister.

Through the remainder of November, I continued to check on the lynx spider family, and I feared the worst when we received our first hard frost. But when I checked on them that morning, gently brushing the flower cluster where the family resided, I was pleasantly surprised to see the mother's legs move and some of her offspring shift around. I did note that there seemed to be far fewer spiderlings at home. No doubt some left the nest to ride out the winter elsewhere, but I suspect others had fallen prey to their siblings since the remaining youngsters were now twice their hatching size, and during all my previous observations, I had not seen the young spiders eat any small insects.

Today, after a few more frosts and a couple of cold rains, only a few youngsters remain in their silken nest. And their mother, once a vibrant jade-green and full-bodied spider, is now in her twilight days a pale tan-green color, and a mere shadow of her former stature. She moves very little when I brush her webbing. In coming days I will find her gone; but I look forward to next year, because in her place, I expect there will be at least one of her young lynx, readying to take her mother's place in the garden.

New Year's Explore

JANUARY 1996 I make an extra effort on New Year's Day to spend as much time as possible exploring the outdoors, hoping that doing so might help predict what the coming year will bring. So this past New Year's, I hung around near my back yard and poked in puddles, ditches, logs, mulch piles, and about everywhere else I could find.

The first place I looked into was one of my mulch piles. I didn't consciously set out to do any mulch pile excavation, it just kind of happened. It began when I dumped a bunch of potato peelings on top of it. The fresh scraps looked out of place there, so I used a stick from another pile and began scraping nearly composted material on top of them. In the process, I uncovered a half-dozen or more cream-colored millipedes.

At first, I thought the curled-up invertebrates may have been beetle larvae, so I caught one to feed to the newts I have in a winter breeding pool. But as soon as I picked it up, I saw it wasn't a tasty beetle, but rather an acrid-smelling and foul-tasting millipede that no self-respecting newt—itself a pretty nasty-tasting thing—would ever want to eat. The millipedes I uncovered are normally rusty-brown-colored, but these specimens were pale because they had just molted their hard, inflexible outer skeleton. As this exoskeleton expands and hardens, it darkens to their normal brown color.

Finding so many millipedes in the same place, all recently molted, can provoke many thoughts and questions. Do millipedes always molt with the onset of winter? And if so, for what reason? I wondered if the soft outer skeleton allowed their internal organs to expand with cold, without causing the skeleton to split. Or, as with a lot of arthropods (including crabs and lobsters), do the female millipedes have to molt prior to mating? That might be plausible since I do find lots of small juvenile millipedes in the early spring. So maybe January is millipede breeding season.

I couldn't spend too much time dwelling on the deceivingly palatable-looking millipedes, because I soon discovered another mulch pile inhabitant that the newts, and some other charges of mine, would definitely like to eat: earthworms. There were bunches of them. The worms were chilled down by the recent cold rain we received, so they were easy to catch. I placed several of them in the potato peel bag and set out to the newt pool to feed them off.

I hadn't given the worms more than a cursory look at first, but when I pulled out the first one I was surprised to see how pink it was. The other worms were a typical worm color: grey-green, with just a glint of blue-green iridescence when the sun caught them just right. But this one worm, a small one, about the diameter of a pencil lead and less than two inches long—perfect food for a newt—really stood out, almost alarmingly, the more I looked at it. The pink body was nearly transparent, and its large blood vessels showed clearly through the skin. What was really alerting were the dozens of tiny whitish things I could see in its tissues. I didn't know if the globular-looking structures were eggs from a parasite, fatty cysts, or something else. Whatever they were, they didn't look good, and I was facing my first ecological dilemma of the year. Do I feed the worm to the newts—an act that could kill the possible parasites, or alternatively help them actually complete their life cycle, to the detriment of the newts—or do I let the worm go back into the mulch pile, an act that could spread whatever disease it seemed to have to other nearby creatures? I considered my options as I fed off the healthy-looking worms, and decided at last to opt on the side of prudence. I removed the sickly worm from the yard by feeding it to a large, worm-eating planarian living under a board.

This particular planarian—an elastic-bodied animal with a head reminiscent of a hammerhead shark, is an Asian exotic that eats creatures including slugs, snails, and worms. While I find this invasive predator interesting as an exotic with few enemies other than a larger planarian, I worry about detrimental consequences this species may have on our native worms. So, yes, maybe I fed this planarian a sick earthworm, knowing in the back of my mind that I may be doing so to its detriment. What will result from this act, I can't begin to guess. But wondering about predator-prey relationships and consequences, especially at the trophic level of worms, is something I look forward to during this new year.

Therapy in Bird Feeding

JANUARY 1989 Many psychologists believe that an aquarium full of fish in the house is good for your nerves. Maybe it's the subtle gurgling sound of air bubbles in the water, reminding us of a babbling brook, or maybe the fluid movements of the fish that offer our eyes some easy distractions. Whatever the reason, aquariums seem to be resurging in popularity.

I prefer a different kind of distraction. To me, there's nothing as relaxing as looking out my living room and kitchen windows and watching the procession of birds visiting our feeding stations.

As with aquariums, there are some duties to be performed in the service of birds, but really not very much labor. The feeders have to be filled, usually once a day (sometimes twice on exceptionally cold days), and the bathing pool has to be kept clean and filled with fresh water, but that's about it. Nothing too extraneous, because unlike fish in an aquarium, birds can go elsewhere in search of food. Still, diligent attention to these simple duties is required, if you want to keep the birds around.

I use a mixture of black oil sunflower and white striped sunflower in all my feeders but one, which consists of only thistle seed, the favorite of very small birds, including the American goldfinch. The standard wild bird seed mix is okay, but sunflower seed seems to be the food of choice for most of the birds visiting my feeders. I usually just throw the seed mix out on the ground for mourning doves to scratch for.

The more time you can commit to watching your feeders, the more you will become involved with them. What that means is, the birds that visit on a regular basis will become familiar to you. You might begin to recognize individuals or small flocks; before long, you'll have a schedule of when certain birds arrive.

Each morning, the first to arrive at my smallest window feeder is a resident Carolina wren. I believe it's one that nested in an old coffee can in my shed last spring and summer. The wren picks at the small black-oil sunflower seeds, in search of kernels that aren't wrapped in their husk. I seldom see the wren actually eat any seed, but rather it just appears to flick the stuff out of the feeder and onto the ground. Maybe it hopes to find an insect in the seeds, since insects are the wren's favorite food. Whatever it's doing, the usually aggressive wren moves off when the next early riser shows up: a Carolina chickadee.

Along with the chickadee come tufted titmice. Before long, purple finches show up, throwing their slightly larger stature around; they dominate the feeder by just sitting on the perches and not giving way. That changes when my pair of northern cardinals show up, the bright red male usually appearing only after the less gaudy female has checked things out. The cardinals too can be domineering, but as with all the birds, they come and go, and nobody is really left out.

I've had only one blue jay take up residence around the feeders, and contrary to their bad reputation, this one doesn't push everyone else away nearly as much as the finches do. This is why it helps to use more than one feeder, so the smaller, more timid birds can have a place to call their own.

The real climax bird at the station is a beautiful red-bellied woodpecker that usually comes blowing in after the rest of the birds have been busy feeding for some time. I'm sure it's the same bird each day, because it appears at about the same time each day. I'm also sure the timely woodpecker is just there for a whistle stop in its busy day. That's fine by me, so long as he, along with the other winged commuters, does stop. I would feel crushed if I put out a banquet and no one dined on it.

Even if the feeders are still full with seeds, all of the birds are usually gone by midmorning, except for the wrens. At first I thought of the birds as a disjunctive group that happened to just ramble by; but, seeing the same species return in similar numbers each midafternoon, I was convinced that their procession is well orchestrated, including as a kind of solo performer the red-bellied woodpecker, following the lovely opening act provided by the cardinal duo.

A Warbler's Encounter

JANUARY 2002 Recently I was watching a large flock of yellow-rumped warblers when suddenly the calm of the moment was interrupted. The little gray-and-yellow-colored warblers in my front yard were carrying on in a very high-spirited fashion, chattering and calling back and forth; they paid little attention to me as I sat motionless, and even when I did move, the tiny birds seemed to be too wrapped up in their own comings and goings to worry about me.

As I watched the warblers mingle amid the branches of the large sycamore near my driveway, several of them descended to the prickly-leafed branches of an American holly tree adorned with bright red berries. I thought they might be interested in eating some of the berries, to supplement their otherwise insectivorous diet, but none of them paused to even look at one.

Some of the warblers felt safe enough in the holly's protective foliage to actually perch quietly on some of the low-hanging branches and preen their feathers. I imagined the little birds felt secure against the threat of snakes, because the weather was cold, but I wasn't sure if birds could reason that far. I'm sure they did figure themselves safe from aerial

47

predators such as small hawks and falcons, both of which make a habit of blowing past the bird-feeding station not far from where the warblers were resting. When our resident Cooper's hawk decides to flush the feeder's occupants, the small birds dart away in a feathery explosion that is quite a sight to witness.

But safe in the confines of thick and spiny holly leaves, these placid warblers seemed at ease—that is, until another kind of predator came rushing in. It was a house cat. It looked like some exotic wild cat, with faint gray and brown stripes across a rather neutral tan background. The cat bounded in a flash after a lone warbler poised near the tip of one of the holly branches. The bird must have seen the cat's movement at the last instant; with an alarmed chatter, it took flight, along with the rest of the flock. The cat, suddenly confused by the rush of so many birds, spun on its tracks, saw me looking at it, and in a panic, took off running before I could move a muscle.

I was able to see that it was wearing a collar, so it had to be somebody's pet, or at least former pet. It struck me that, had I been one of those birds, I wouldn't have had a chance to escape; unlike wild birds that must be ever on the alert for danger, I had been casually focusing my attention on one small spot in the holly tree.

I was relieved to see that the flock of warblers, along with two mourning doves and a cardinal I hadn't seen before the cat's arrival, had all managed to fly to safety. And then I remembered the blue jay that had not been so lucky just two days before. The jay was feeding near the ground just below one of our feeders, and apparently not paying close atten-tion to its surroundings, when it fell victim to this same cat.

I came on the scene moments after the earlier incident and startled the cat with a loud shout.

I know it sounds strange, but something about a house cat killing songbirds bothers me more than the thought of a hawk doing so. I think it's because house cats, or at least domestic house cats, don't need to kill birds to survive. Wild hawks do. House cats are fantastic hunters and credited as being the world's most efficient mammalian predator of songbirds, and as such, they're responsible for bringing several bird species to the verge of extinction.

As I watched the suite of songbirds returning to my yard just moments after the cat unceremoniously departed, I thought about the new threats songbirds face in our suburban neighborhoods: along with cats, they have to be wary of kids with BB guns. Our wildlife protection laws prohibit indiscriminate killing of native songbirds such as warblers and cardinals. It's illegal to shoot songbirds, or take their eggs, or even damage their active nests. To allow otherwise would certainly bring peril to many species already threatened by habitat loss. If we really care about birds, we need to exercise restraint on our cats' predisposition to catch and eat them—not because we want to punish our cats, but because it's the right thing to do, for the birds.

Nest Box Interloper

JANUARY 2005 About a month ago my son Carson discovered an adorable little flying squirrel sleeping in one of the bluebird nest boxes we had attached to a pine tree near our house. A week later, he discovered a small, furry brown bat sleeping contentedly in a similar box, this one attached to a wooden post located less than a hundred feet from the pine-tree box. Last spring and summer the pine-tree box provided nesting space for two lovely pairs of great crested flycatchers, which had insisted on decorating the inch-and-a-half diameter entrance with strands of pine straw that they carefully placed to hang out the hole like a bit of taffeta announcing their occupancy.

The box on the post was used first by a pair of eastern bluebirds, and then by a pair of very pushy Carolina chickadees that moved in the moment the bluebirds' offspring fledged. That was after I added two other boxes on the opposite side of our house in an effort to draw away the interloping chickadees. The two pairs of birds squabbled until early August, when they both finally moved out.

The boxes remained vacant until sometime in autumn, when the flying squirrel and bat moved in. I hoped for them to use the boxes as winter quarters, and they might actually have settled in to stay, had it not been for the single-minded determination of one red-bellied woodpecker that took it upon himself to renovate the boxes to suit his needs— namely, by chiseling all around the entry hole with his specialized bill keenly adapted for the purpose of excavating wood.

In short order, what once had been a neatly bored one-and-a-half-inch diameter opening was expanded to a rough-edged gape more than two inches wide. That wouldn't have been too large for either the bat or the flying squirrel, I'm sure, but the incessant hammering they had to endure proved too loud for both mammals, and soon after the woodpecker began his work they left to find new winter homes, the bat first, and then the squirrel.

Of course, now that the woodpecker's work is done to his satisfaction, he too has taken leave of what had been his all-consuming work. In fact, the woodpecker's passion for his trade was not lost on any of the four boxes I had spread around our house, as evidenced by the enlarged openings in the front door of each box.

I might have thwarted the busy woodpecker by placing a metal rim around each bird box entrance. But so long as that woodpecker had something to occupy his talents at woodworking, my thought was, at least my *own* house would be spared his attentions.

Pileated Party

FEBRUARY 2001 February is National Wild Bird Feeding Month, and though the celebration has just begun, I've already been richly rewarded for my backyard efforts. I was peering into the winter-clear water of one of my bog ponds when I suddenly realized how noisy the woods around me were. The trees and shrubs were literally aflutter with the comings and goings of dozens of small songbirds of several species, including one not-so-small individual that I could hear scrabbling up the trunk of a fair-sized loblolly pine tree. I knew it was a woodpecker of some sort because its climbing sounds were punctuated every so often by a tell-tale methodical hammering sound.

As I searched for the woodpecker among a tangle of dead vines hanging from the pine, I started to watch the littler birds around me. The most common were yellow-rumped warblers, named after the bright yellow patch on the base of their tails; they're also known as myrtle warblers, because they eat wax myrtle berries, especially in winter when their favorite foods—small insects and spiders—are hard to come by. The warblers were flitting amidst the myrtle branches, casually picking at the BB-sized fruits of the evergreen shrubs.

Pileated woodpecker, *Dryocopus pileatus*

These warblers were joined by a pair of steel-gray tufted titmice and a number of Carolina chickadees. The titmice and chickadees were clambering through the tangle of greenbrier and old wisteria vines hanging from the pine tree, where I continued to hear but not see the working woodpecker. I enjoyed the chickadees' acrobatics, which included hanging upside down as they searched furrows and cracks in the surfaces of the vines.

The small birds remained close to the woodpecker, which I had yet to see. It seemed like they were staying nearby in hopes that one of the bark chips the woodpecker loosened might carry some tasty morsel, like a fat beetle grub or spider.

I crept toward the pine cautiously to avoid frightening the animal before getting a good look at it, and my reward came when the bird sidled around the tree, coming into an almost full view, save for the drapery of vines. As I had suspected, the bird turned out to be a handsome adult pileated woodpecker, a nearly crow-sized bird that I've been trying to coax to our yard for years. The tree it was working happened to be one of the treats I'd hoped would do the trick.

Pileated woodpeckers are powerful birds, equipped with a nearly two-inch-long chisel-shaped bill for chipping bark and excavating nest cavities especially in dead wood. They're striking to look at—their large crimson head crest stands out against their jet-black body plumage, and their crisp white underwing feathers flash dramatically when they take flight.

February is the time when male and female pileated woodpeckers form pair bonds as a precursor to mating and to raising offspring, a task that requires the efforts of both birds. Nest excavation, usually in a large dead or hollow tree, begins in March, accompanied by loud drumming and high-pitched *kuk-kuk* calls to identify the pair's territory.

I assumed this bird was after food, rather than a nest site, because it seemed bent only on peeling bark away from a large part of the tree. I'm certain that the treats it sought under the bark were cream-colored, soft-bodied beetle larvae, especially long-horned beetles whose larvae feed on the dead and dying wood located just beneath the outer tree bark. I find them all the time while messing under logs, and judging from this particular bird's activity, I have to assume it was having success or else it would have moved on.

Pileated woodpeckers chip away at logs on the ground and dead trees standing in the woods, and, like other woodpeckers, they use their barbed tongues to spear the soft grubs they find. It's a lot of work, really, as evidenced by this individual's efforts that I was lucky enough to observe.

Adult pileated woodpeckers weigh a little more than half a pound. If they're like most birds, they probably need to eat about ten percent of their body weight every day to fuel their activities and their metabolism. That equates to about an ounce of grubs and other rich morsels every day. Each grub it catches probably weighs about one-third of a gram, so that adds up to about eighty or ninety medium-sized grubs per day. These are round figures, of course, but even if the bird had to catch half that number, I can say from my own experiences looking for grubs in dead logs that it requires considerable effort; you have to examine a lot of logs and trees. So, if you have trouble appreciating a yard with old logs on the ground or if you don't like dead trees, instead of hauling them off or chopping them down, think about leaving them where they are—the pileated woodpeckers will appreciate them for you.

After the Burn: A Rebirth

FEBRUARY 2004 Recently I participated in the North Carolina Forest Service's Fire Wise program, which is designed to help property owners reduce the risks associated with wildfire. Our new home is located within a drastically different ecosystem from the salt-marsh habitat we previously lived alongside. It's tucked inside a longleaf-pine savanna that sits adjacent to a large tract of open land (arguably one of the highest fire hazard habitats in North America). Our property was a perfect candidate to serve as a pilot Fire Wise project.

The pilot project was a prescribed fuel-reduction burn in a rural interface. The Fire Wise program in other states is often applied in urban interface settings where houses are clustered closely together, often nestled among large trees and other plants that can transfer heat and flame to nearby structures in the event of a wildfire on adjacent wild land, hence the term "interface."

Our prescribed burn came off picture-perfect. Nearly two decades free of fire, our savanna was knee-deep in volatile fuel: dense wire grass, pine straw, and various small shrubs. Historically, natural longleaf-pine savanna habitats get swept over by lightning-sparked fires every few years. The fires consume the accumulated pine straw and burns (but rarely kills) clumps of grass and shrubs in a natural phenomenon that allows sun-loving wildflowers and groundcovers to flourish. Without fire, the savanna can give way to woody vegetation that grows into thickets and, eventually, mixed pine and hardwood forest habitat. In our unique part of the world, fire-adapted savanna plants make up a who's-who list including many species found nowhere else on the planet: Venus' flytrap and Carolina goldenrod, to name but two.

I watched in amazement as the purposely set fires ran through our property in orderly lines ignited by the Forest Service fire managers. I'm familiar with the prescribed burning process and intimate with the habitat, but I was awed nonetheless by the sight of long lines of low, creeping flames engulfing everything in their path. Clumps of stringy wire grass two feet wide vanished in mere seconds, along with pine straw gathered in loose layers around the bases of head-high pine saplings. Still, wire grass is so fire-adapted that only a few seconds after the fire had crawled over the grassy mounds, I could run my bare hand through the black stubble and detect very little evidence of heat.

The same was true for the seedling longleaf pines, whose one- to six-foot-tall stems had had their needles scorched off and outer bark blackened by the flames. The needles of the longleaf pine protect the tree's main trunk and tender growing tips by serving as sacrificial heat-absorbers that prevent the flame from damaging underlying growth cells. I didn't have to worry about the grasses or pines, because for them, this fire was just what nature would have ordered. The largest difference between our fire and a natural fire is, we decided where and when to burn.

Less than an hour after the fire was completed, I walked around the blackened savanna, stepping between small stands of black stubble that hours earlier had been mop-head-like clumps of blond grass. As the fire burned, I had seen numerous large grasshoppers fly from the danger zone, but not all of them made it to safety; now, I saw several dead and stunned grasshoppers lying about on the scorched ground, and just as I was lamenting their loss, a large flock of black crows whisked in, noisily caw-cawing to one another as they began to scour the scene for easy treats. I watched and listened to the animated crows walking about, making satisfied crow noises as they gobbled up every last grasshopper they could find.

I had some concern for other small creatures in the path of the savanna fire, including the many spiders that lived there. But I learned the following evening that my concern was not warranted. While walking about the transformed savanna, admiring a flock of busy robins working the remaining leaf litter, I turned toward the lowering sun, and the angled light caught thousands of crisscrossing strands of spider webs that seemed to completely cover the ground. Each strand defined a path some small spider had taken earlier, showing clear evidence that life in the savanna was quickly resuming, just as it had done for thousands of years and countless past generations.

Burning the savanna around our home was done to help protect our property, but it was also done for the sake of the fire-dependent savanna itself. The tapestry of spider silk I saw draped across the ground signified a rejuvenation that only fire can produce in such a hallowed habitat as the longleaf-pine savanna. It may be called a rebirth, but I think "revival" is a more fitting name for what we've done at nature's behest.

2

Just Down the Road

A Surprise Package

JULY 1995 I was in my office at the North Carolina Aquarium, diligently juggling several tasks at one time, when much to my delight, one of the staff approached my doorway clutching a small plastic food container in her hands. I knew instantly that the container was not being used as originally intended because its top was perforated with numerous small holes. At once, I hung up the phone mid-dial, turned away from the computer screen, and set aside the notepad I was referencing messages from; my attention was diverted from these multiple activities and singularly focused on that simple, opaque plastic box. A small container with tiny holes poked in its lid is like one of those internationally recognizable direction signs—it reads: Live Animal Inside.

I've seen and peered into more jars, boxes, buckets, bags, and other implements of containment than I could ever count, but few things elicit such an immediate sense of wonder from me as a common kitchen container with air holes punched in its top.

So there I was, turning my back to the rest of the world all because a little plastic box showed up at my doorway. In this instance, the bearer wasn't sure what she had, but I was confident the animal inside wasn't dangerous because of something she said before I could get a good look: "They were flying around under a parking lot lamp."

Now, I've had frogs jump out of various containers more than once without warning, as well as chipmunks, lizards, birds, and squirrels. There was a particularly memorable experience many years ago with a striped skunk in a large cardboard box, which still haunts me today. So now I pick up on subtle clues when it comes to opening surprise packages—like a declaration from the carrier: "I think it bites," or "It jumps," or "It flies." So in this case I figured anything flying around a parking lot couldn't be too great a threat. I peeled the top back gingerly, savoring the moment, my mind reeling image after image of what might possibly be inside.

With the top mostly off I could see crumpled paper inside but no animal. Then suddenly the paper moved, and I could see legs—jointed legs—each with a pair of small hooks at their end. I was looking at some kind of insect, and, judging by the size of its appendages, I knew it was an insect of considerable stature. I carefully lifted the wrinkled paper to try and see the animal's body, and, to my delight, two spectacular female unicorn beetles emerged. Each was about an inch-and-a-half long and nearly an inch across the back. Its shiny, armorlike exoskeleton was pea-soup green, flecked with delicate black specks as though dabbed by a fine-tip ink marker. When I picked one of them up, it gripped my fingers tenaciously with its strong leg hooks and breathed quiet sighs of indignation that sounded like one of those old-fashioned perfume sprayers being squeezed.

Unicorn beetles get their name from the male's large, forward-pointing "horn" on the front of his thorax. A smaller

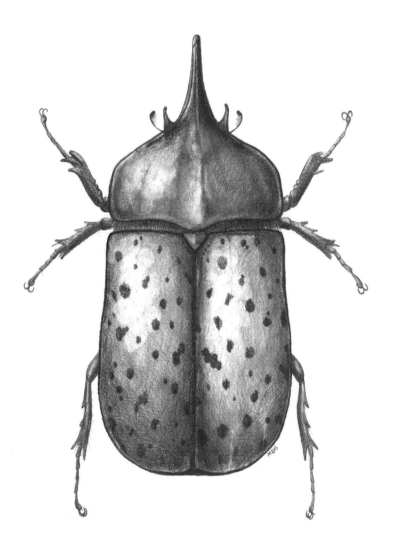

Unicorn beetle, *Dynastes tityus*

"horn" arcs up from the top of his head, giving the impression that the two horns combine to make a set of pincers. The horns can mesh together when the male lifts his head, and the pinch they produce is strong enough to alarm the uninitiated.

I was ecstatic at the beetles' arrival because I had a lovely pair of male and female unicorn beetles at home in a terrarium full of rotting logs, this particular beetle's favorite food and habitat. I replaced the now calmed insect back into its temporary container and secured the top, filled with that same sense one gets after opening a gift. The unexpected present occupied my mind the rest of the day, and, much to the beetles' chagrin, they were hoisted out for examination each time someone noted the conspicuous container on my desk.

The beetles' stay in my office was brief. That afternoon I placed them in the established beetle terrarium at home, where they busily sequestered themselves, along with the two I already had, in the damp recesses of the rotting wood at the bottom of the tank. I later released the lot of them into a much larger log pile, in hopes that a colony might get established—a colony that could in future years provide my two curious young sons with one more living wonder to watch and celebrate, should they ever have the chance to find one to bring to me, maybe in a small box with holes poked in the top.

Mud Dauber Delight

JULY 1994 Venomous animals are some of the most intriguing creatures you could hope to observe. Fortunately for me, southeastern North Carolina has an abundant selection to choose from, including a few snakes, several kinds of spiders, and an incredible host of ants, bees, hornets, and wasps.

Among my favorites of these venomous hunters are the members of the solitary wasp clan, which make their living hunting insects and spiders to use as food for their developing offspring.

The most recent of these observations came about accidentally, after I found a spider wasp nest tube. The nest tube was a column of mud plastered to the side of a wall. The wasp that made the nest was a metallic blue-black color, about an inch long, sporting shiny black wings and long, thin legs.

The nest column itself was constructed of fine, ochre-colored mud and clay. The whole structure was about nine inches long and about three-fourths of an inch wide. In three places the column had been broken open, and I could see the empty egg-shaped cocoon inside that had once contained the wasp's developing pupa. I presumed the rest of the nest tube was empty and thought I'd do no harm in prying it off the wall for a closer look. But when I worked my knife blade under it, the clay wall cracked and a big piece of it fell away, along with the contents that had been held inside. I realized that my presumption was incorrect, and that I had broken into an active nursery chamber.

The chamber contents turned out to be spiders—but not just any spiders. I counted twenty-two on the ground, from BB-size up to the diameter of a pea. That the wasp had gone to the trouble of collecting twenty-two spiders for her offspring's larder was in itself impressive, but what really stunned me was that the spiders were all black widows. The two biggest of them had already been eaten by the fat, caterpillar-like wasp larva. All that remained of them were their legs and hard cephalothorax (the body part where the legs and head attach). The soft abdomen had been nearly completely consumed.

I'll admit that I felt a little uneasy with twenty-two black widows at my feet, even though they were paralyzed by the female wasp's venom. They were still alive—just incapable of moving.

As I picked through the immobilized spiders, the female wasp returned to find her nest chamber opened. She pretty much ignored me and seemed confused about what to do for her larva. She appeared to try for a while to position the larva down in the remains of the tube, but after a few minutes she stopped moving it with her jaws and suddenly just pushed it out, unfortunately with fatal results to the larva. She then proceeded to remove four more spiders from the broken chamber, bringing the total number of black widows she had caught to twenty-six. My sense of guilt at having caused the untimely loss of the wasp larva was in some ways overshadowed by my sense of wonder about this discovery. Were the remaining chambers stocked only with black widow spiders? Would the offspring from this female seek only black widow spiders to stock their own offspring's nursery larder?

Black widow spiders are highly venomous creatures whose bite may cause death even to an animal as large as a human. And while black widows certainly serve an important function in the environment, it's nice to know that there is something other than bug spray at work to ensure their numbers are kept in check—even if it is a wasp with a venomous sting.

The Joy of Clamming

AUGUST 1988 Recreational clamming is one of the few distractions in our area that yield direct, tangible rewards. To some, the idea of clamming conjures up images of muddy salt-marsh flats, sharp-edged oyster shells, and menacing blue crabs. And these things are certainly all present where clams live, but I've discovered that there are many more treats in store for the observant clammer.

To prepare for clamming, you'll need a clam rake (or four-pronged garden rake), a bucket, a pair of old sneakers, and a marsh flat. When you find the salt marsh, observe the woody plant growth along the marsh border. The three dominant types of trees there are the live oak, the yaupon, and the wax myrtle. To survive in this area, trees and shrubs must be salt-tolerant and strong enough to resist the almost constant winds that blow along the coast. These three woody plants grow tightly together and are interwoven with the twinning stems of greenbrier vines. All combined, when growing on relic dunes near the ocean, they form a dense mass of vegetation known as a maritime forest. Maritime forests are valuable habitats for many kinds of animals, especially during the winter months when food is scarce. Several kinds of seed- and berry-eating birds winter in the forest, feeding on the bright red clusters of yaupon berries and the black berries of the greenbrier vine.

Press on through this narrow band of forest and you'll eventually arrive at the marsh to begin clamming. Choosing a suitable clamming area is simple. Find a salt marsh that's open by public access—look to be sure there are no signs declaring the area closed to shellfishing—and also look to see if anyone else is clamming there. One sign of a good clamming spot is the presence of other clammers, but if no one else is there, go for it anyway.

Once you've tested the waters to determine depth and temperature, place your bucket where the tide won't carry it away, and begin raking. Hard clams, or quahogs as the Native Americans called them, spend most of their time just under the surface of the mud. Digging deep is usually not necessary. Simply scrape the surface down to about two inches and you'll be surprised at what you find.

When I'm out clamming, I usually find fewer clams than most people do. This isn't because I don't look for them, but because I get distracted easily, knowing each clump of oysters I encounter may hold some secretive creature inside. I always have to investigate; even small clumps of oysters are themselves tiny ecosystems. On close examination (and you will have to look really close for most co-habitators), you might see a heavy-clawed crab known as a mud crab. This crab, a relative of the stone crab, spends its time searching for food in the cracks and crevices created by fused oyster shells. It is a very secretive crustacean, and when you pick up an oyster cluster, these shy crabs retreat to the deepest recess they can find.

You also might find limpets growing on the oysters. Limpets are snail-like animals that slowly graze over hard surfaces, scraping away algae with their file-like mouthpart. Barnacles also find oysters to be a good surface to grow on. These odd crustaceans close up their shells when exposed at low tide, but when submerged at high tide they open up and wave their feathery legs to sweep the plankton to their mouth. If you're careful, before you disturb the oyster clump, look at it for a while in the water and see if a small fish is lurking within. Gobies, blennies, baby spadefish, and many others use oyster clumps for shelter.

You may notice as you explore the marsh with your rake that the mud flat is coated with a thin layer of pale green surface mud. This layer is almost odorless, and it gets its color from light-loving diatoms and single-celled algae. But just below this layer, the marsh mud is black and quite smelly. The familiar "low tide" smell of the marsh is caused by hydrogen sulfide–producing bacteria that occur naturally in the marsh sediment. The odor is similar to that of a rotten egg, though these bacteria aren't harmful to humans and you needn't worry about getting the mud on your hands.

If you put a little piece of the green surface mud in your bucket and sift it around a bit, you might find a number of bright red worms. These elongate mud inhabitants are known as polychaete worms. Most are predators of smaller worms and other tiny soft-bodied animals.

If you do decide to dig deep in the mud—remembering to be careful of the sharp-edged oysters—you might find a thin-shelled bivalve known as the false razor clam. This relative of the hard clam is very common in the marsh mud, and it is one of the cherished meals of the American oyster-catcher, a large black-and-white shorebird that prowls the mud flats looking for clams and other bivalves to eat. The oystercatcher removes the clam's soft body by inserting its oyster-knife-like bill between the partially opened shells of a filter-feeding bivalve. After clipping the muscles that hold the shells together, the oystercatcher slurps down its prize and sets off in search of another. If you see a lot of empty false razor shells on the mud flat, there's a good chance an oystercatcher was having a meal.

But back to your clamming efforts. Even if you don't find any live clams, you can still find reward in the shells that abound in the marsh. If you find a set of shell halves together, close them tight and look to see if there are chips broken off around the clam shell edge. Broken chips are a sign that a large whelk or conch opened up and ate the clam before you could. The whelk is a giant snail with a big rubbery foot that it uses to grasp the clam while it uses its own shell edges to leverage the halves of the clam shell apart. That's how the chips happen. It's a slow process, and likely not pleasant for the clam, especially when the whelk inserts its file-like tongue, or radula, to scrape and grind the clam's soft parts as it eats.

Maybe we should just look for clam shells, since live clams have it hard enough with all the other things looking to eat them. If you find empty shells with a beautiful purple region inside, they're from the northern quahog; the southern quahog generally lacks the purple coloration. In past times, this purple shell material was cherished by Native Americans. They would grind away the surrounding white parts, creating little disks of purple shell, which they strung together and, in so doing, created the first true American currency: wampum. So, whether or not you find live clams, at least you know that clamming can always be a productive venture.

Seaturtles in the Storm

AUGUST 1994 It was one of those scenes in nature that almost seems contrived. I received a report that a seaturtle nest in Kure Beach was being exposed by high tide waves and a few hatchling turtles and unhatched eggs were being washed into the surf. From the description of where the nest was located I figured it would be a cinch to find, but the nest eluded my search. Then the next day, long after I wrote the story off, another report came in about, supposedly the same nest. So I again headed out, this time with a better description of the location, and after a hike of about two hundred yards I was able to find the exposed nest.

Loggerhead seaturtles build their nests in beach sand above the normal high tide line, usually at the base of the frontal dune line. Quite often the turtles time their nesting to coincide with the full moon, because full-moon high tides tend to be higher than other high tides, allowing the awkward turtles an easier crawl up the beach. Once the nest site is chosen, the big turtle digs in her hind flippers and proceeds to scoop out a chamber about ten to twenty-four inches deep to lay her eggs in. Once egg laying is completed, she covers the nest dutifully, turns toward the sea, and departs—digging and covering the nest is the extent of her parental care.

I expected to find the nest I was looking for right under my feet. But heavy winds and surf, coupled with a full-moon high tide, had caused such intense sand erosion that the stretch of beach where a turtle had crawled up two months ago was now cut away to a depth of five feet or more. The beach profile stretched from the water line where the waves receded across a narrow band of level sand, and then the level beach stopped dramatically at a vertical wall of sand that was clearly a recently eroded cross section of the frontal dune. The high tide was almost full when I got to the beach and the storm waves were just beginning to lap at the base of the sand wall, where the nest was exposed.

If the nest had been any further seaward of the sheer wall, it would have already been lost. But as loggerhead luck would have it, the erosion stopped along a line that perfectly bisected the nest, and the only reason I found the nest at all was a single egg I'd seen, slightly larger than a golf ball, protruding out from the wall right at eye level!

Watching the waves encroach up the nest, I had to make an immediate decision about how to remove the eggs, a responsibility that came with my membership in the North Carolina Sea Turtle Rescue Network. With waves more than gently lapping at my feet, I began delicately removing pieces of eggshells. The shells were thin and papery, unlike the hard shell of a bird. It was apparent that the nest had contained dozens of eggs, most already hatched, but I did find eight firm, intact white eggs and eleven indented, yellowish ones. The yellow eggs were probably infertile; the white ones, I hoped, just hadn't hatched yet.

The best sight was the discovery of two recently hatched turtles. I suppose my hasty excavation came as a shock to the two-inch-long reptiles that had been at one moment in total darkness, at the next in blinding sunlight. Both turtle hatchlings carried the remainder of what had been a yolk sac, so I knew they had only begun to dig their way out of the nest. I released one immediately into the ocean, and without a second look back it slipped into the waves and disappeared. Its nestmate would soon follow on its own long journey to the Gulf Stream a day or two later, after its yolk sac fell off.

I collected the remaining intact eggs in a box, which I then placed, along with a bit of their natal beach sand, in an incubation tray at the aquarium. In a matter of just a few days the eggs hatched, and soon after, the hatchling turtles dropped the remains of their yolk sacs. I gladly released them back onto the beach to follow a time-honored path into the Atlantic—a path they would not have been able to begin had their nest not been discovered by an observant and concerned beachgoer who felt compelled to report the finding in hopes that something might be done to help.

Toil the Ant

AUGUST 1998 While sitting in the shade of an oak tree near a friend's driveway, I couldn't help but notice the hasty movements of several very small ants. It was a hot day, and the ants were doggedly traversing the pits and craters of the asphalt pavement. I recognized the insects as a common variety of field ant, though the exact species was unknown to me. Each ant was less than one-eighth of an inch long and its three body parts—head, thorax, and abdomen—were each about the size of a grain of sugar. These were very small ants.

What most amazed me about them was the speed at which they carried themselves over the sun-baked pavement. I tried doing some comparative guesswork to translate their rate to human activity, based on relative body size. Like, if an ant is one-eighth of an inch long and it travels twelve inches in four seconds—which is about what these ants were doing—how fast would that be for a six-foot-tall human? It was a fun math exercise, so I timed a few of the ants and determined that they were covering ninety-six times their body length in four seconds; or, more simply, the ants were moving at twenty-four times their length in one second. To match that feat, if my math is correct, a six-foot-tall human with, let's say, a five-foot running stride would have to run 120 feet per second!

Following this mental teaser, I decided to interact with the little beasties by offering them a crumb of bread from my peanut butter and marmalade sandwich. The tidbit was slightly smaller than a grain of dried rice, and moist from the marmalade. I initially placed it on the asphalt in front of me to see how long it would take for an ant to find it. That question was answered in less than ten seconds, and just as quickly, I found myself wondering what the ants would do with the sweet treat once they found it. I assumed it would be too large for them, and that they would have to divide it up to carry it off. To my surprise, the first ant to find it took charge of its windfall discovery by picking up the whole thing in its jaws and trotting off with it. The bread piece must have weighed several times the ant's own bodyweight, and yet the ant still trundled off, albeit with some difficulty, under the burden of its prize.

I now had myself in a predicament. I'd invested about ten minutes in watching these ants do little more than scamper around, and now that one of them was on task with a mission, I couldn't walk away and ignore what would happen next.

So I continued to endure the heat as I watched the little ant navigate the rough asphalt terrain, occasionally bumping into a fellow ant along the way. After about a minute of determined progress, the small ant allowed another of its kin to take over the burden. The transfer reminded me of images of our early Pony Express. After some bit of load adjusting, the new ant resumed the trek, though it was now clear that it was trying to maneuver off the pavement and up into the planting bed where I was sitting. The bed was edged by old railroad timbers, a ten-inch climb the ant—carrying a prize many times its own weight—was able to accomplish without mishap. Once on the summit, the plucky insect forged ahead into the tangle of dry pine needles that covered the planter bed, negotiating one needle after another like an ironworker on a skyscraper.

Six minutes had elapsed since the first ant had grabbed the bread crumb, and in that time the crumb had moved about twelve feet, carried by three different relay ants. My curiosity was now piqued, as I didn't yet know the location of the ant's nest. I couldn't stop watching, even though friends and family were beginning to wonder where I had gotten off to. All of a sudden, as the latest relay ant made its way over a pine needle, a quick-footed spider appeared from below; it was a striped grass spider with a leg span about the diameter of a dime. The spider saw the bobbing motion of the bread crumb and, thinking it something palatable, made a gesture toward the hapless ant. But the spider was somehow able to determine that the tantalizing bobbing thing was not edible. It sulked back into its lair, and the ant continued on its way, completely unaware of what had transpired.

It was at this point that my young teenage son Robin showed up, wondering what I was doing. I explained what was happening without taking my eyes off the ant, to keep from losing sight of it in the straw.

The gradual appearance of several more ants indicated that the last leg of the trip was at hand. The burdened ant was greeted by several of its nest mates, which each offered to help with its comrade's chore. Their so-called assistance resulted in more confusion than coordination, and negotiating the final two feet to the nest took as much time as the previous ten feet! But at least the nest was now in sight, a small hole surrounded by a clean dome of reddish sand. The laboring ant, probably the fifth one to participate in the relay, covered the last inches to the hole in a few seconds. It popped down inside, and everyone's ordeal was over.

I was relieved, but probably not as much as the ants, who had so determinedly gone about their chore of acquiring food and transferring it home. As it turned out, the distance the ants covered, beginning with where I originally placed the crumb and ending at their nest, was just over thirty feet. It took them about twenty-five minutes to accomplish the trek. Along the way they skirted several black carpenter ants, much larger than themselves, that no doubt would have seized the chance to abscond the breadcrumb for their own nest. The one little ant also inadvertently dodged a spider that chose not to pursue it. And all these hazards the ants faced in addition to the hot asphalt and twisted tangle of pine straw they had to forge across.

This thirty-foot journey might seem mundane at first. We tend to view what happens in our own back yards as less interesting than what happens in a rain forest or other exotic locales so often portrayed on television. The only difference is that I was outdoors, in a neighbor's front yard, able to watch nature in action, in person, and in real time.

Saga of the Chigger

AUGUST 1999 Chiggers are minute arachnids—mites actually—related to ticks and spiders. The so-called chigger that is a nuisance to people is actually the larval stage of the harvest mite, a name derived from the fact that the creature is found in grain fields, usually at harvest time around late summer and early autumn. While the adult harvest mite makes a living eating tiny insects and their eggs, its larval stage, the chigger, is a parasite on warm-blooded creatures, including us humans.

Adult harvest mites grow to about three millimeters across. Their color is red-brown, and they have eight legs attached to their pear-shaped bodies. The fat end is the abdomen, and the tapered front end is where the head and legs are attached. The eyes and mouthparts of the mites are too small to see without a strong magnifying lens, but that can be said for the whole animal. Their legs are simple affairs with tiny hairs that help them detect other tiny things around it.

My first real encounter with chiggers occurred in Texas during a university-sponsored collecting trip in search of various reptiles, rodents, and bats. Our crew worked through the afternoon and into early dusk setting up fine mesh nets designed to catch bats in much the same way gill nets catch fish. We also set out a number of live traps for the rats and mice we hoped to find. And we identified slabs of rocks and large logs to check for snakes and lizards the following morning.

The setup process had us crisscrossing a large field containing a beautiful stand of big bluestem grass whose billowy, amber-colored seed heads rose six feet tall in places. It was a wonderful area to run around in, with a few stately post oak trees under which we pitched our tents to take advantage of the shade.

As day turned to night, some of us started to itch a little, but no one complained about mosquitoes, so we figured the irritation must have been caused by little pokes and scratches from the grasses. Around two in the morning, though, we were all writhing in agony, itching all over our bodies. And then one crew member identified the cause: chiggers. As they say, "We were eaten up with them."

To understand what it is that actually does the biting, look at the harvest mite's life cycle. Adult harvest mites lay unimaginably tiny eggs in grassy fields and open woodlands. These eggs hatch into the six-legged larvae we call chiggers, which right away climb up into grass to wait for an unsuspecting warm-blooded host to come by. When one does, as we did, the chigger grabs hold with its hooklike legs and then scampers over the host's body, stopping at a constriction point such as an armpit, an elastic band, a belt, or the top of a sock. It stops there to bite its host, secreting a special protein with its saliva that causes plasma to pool inside a miniscule blister, from which the chigger drinks its fill and then drops off, sated, ready to transform to its eight-legged nymph stage.

The chigger's habit of stopping to feed along constriction lines is one helpful way to identify them as the cause of itching bites; however, by the time you detect a chigger bite, the interloper will probably have already fallen away, leaving behind a powerful irritation that resists almost all anti-itch therapies (including fingernail polish, a common practice some use, mistakenly thinking it will kill the antagonist). You should deal with a chigger bite just as you would most other insect bites: try to ignore it and not scratch. Dermatologists do suggest a very hot bath; the heat reacts with the chemicals causing the itch, providing some temporary relief, which is much better than none at all.

My first encounter with chiggers was made even worse by the insulting lack of field-dwelling rodents we worked so hard to find. Looking back on the circumstances, maybe it was because the other warm-blooded creatures had better sense than to go running around in an open grassy field in late summer.

The question invariably comes up after such an experience with one of nature's gifts: What good can there be in chiggers? To answer that question, we must look at the animal's name and its origin. As mentioned earlier, the adult harvest mite feeds on tiny insects and insect eggs, especially aphid eggs, throughout the warm season. The mites lay their eggs in late summer and the eggs hatch into larval chiggers around harvest time, which is when we find them at their best.

So chiggers—or more correctly, adult harvest mites—attack insects that would consume and damage farm crops. Therefore, the harvest mite is an ally in our campaign to grow food to feed the world. Now doesn't that thought help the itch go away?

Eruption of Spadefoot Toads

SEPTEMBER 1999 As my family and I were getting ready for Hurricane Floyd's arrival, we had the chance to visit some friends not far from our house. Their yard was awash in clear rainwater that had backed up from a low area in the woods near them. As we stood in their yard I could hear the wonking nasal sounds of male spadefoot toads calling out for the attention of resident females. The presence of the toads was confirmed by our friends' young daughter, who approached us with a large three-inch specimen she found in a streetside puddle.

The spadefoot toad derives its name from the small, black, spade-like growth on the bottom of each hind foot. The growth is employed as a digging tool to facilitate excavation—this "troglodyte" of toads spends a mostly solitary life underground. The spadefoot toad's fossorial lifestyle, as well as its refusal to breach the surface in daylight, can explain why most people rarely get the chance to see one. The sight of the toads at my friends' house was due in large part to the rains delivered by Hurricane Floyd.

Southeastern North Carolina is home to about twenty-two different kinds of tailless amphibians—otherwise known as frogs and toads. Of these, only three are actually toads. The rest are made up of tree frogs, those little green jewels with suction-cupped toes; true frogs, including such notables as the bullfrog, the green frog, and the leopard frog; and the last frog in our area, in a group all its own: the narrow-mouthed frog, an inch-long subterranean dweller.

Among southeastern North Carolina's three toads, the common southern toad of mushroom and garden fame is often seen loitering under streetlights and other places where insects gather. The less common oak toad inhabits the dry, sandy habitats dominated by longleaf pine and turkey oak—it looks much like its larger southern toad cousin but with a bold white racing stripe running down the middle of its back. And then there is the eastern spadefoot toad.

Close examination reveals that the eastern spadefoot is wrapped in a thin, moist skin lacking the telltale, wart-like bumps that adorn more familiar backyard toads. The eastern spadefoot is usually pale brown in color, with a pair of narrow yellow stripes running the length of its back and another running along each side, just above the belly.

I have always been fond of spadefoot toads, in part because they are seldom seen, and hence a treat to come across; but more because of their disarmingly bulbous golden eyes that stare blankly, through elliptical, catlike black pupils.

While the spadefoot's figure isn't necessarily glamorous, its eyes are nothing short of stunning, even if they evoke an aloofness that seems vacuous. This is a trait shared by all spadefoots, and I believe it's a consequence of their solitary, subterranean disposition. I should mention that spadefoots are not to be handled casually, as their skin secretes a peppery-smelling toxin that tastes even worse than that of their cousin the southern toad. It's a taste that doesn't go away quickly, and most predators foolish enough to try one do so only once. The spadefoot is solitary for most of its life, but not all of it. During heavy, warm rains like those brought on by Floyd, adult male spadefoot toads call from rain pools in unison to carry their courting calls further afield, where more females may hear them. While some other frogs behave in this way, there is a collaborative effort that is unique to the spadefoot. Spadefoot toads breed in temporary rain pools that generally last only a few weeks after a heavy rain fills them. Tadpoles must transform quickly to avoid drying out with the pool. When rain pools shrink and food becomes scarce, spadefoot tadpoles swim in tight clusters, beating their tails to stir the bottom and bring up bits of food. This activity creates a small depression where water may persist for an extra day or two, allowing the tadpoles the necessary time to transform before their nursery pool dries up.

The tiny frogs people began seeing in our area shortly after Floyd's assault were recently transformed toadlets spawned by the adult spadefoot toads we heard during the hurricane: the spadefoot class of 1999. Because spadefoot toad reproduction requires specially timed rain events to reproduce, it is possible that they were the first new generation of this species to come along in several years. We didn't see these toads for more than a few days, because they quickly began burying themselves underground and waiting for nightfall, when they would emerge to search for tiny insect prey amid grasses and leaves. They are definitely a benefit to our species, if only because of the insect control they provide. But more to the point, the spadefoot toad is a member of our diverse community whose lineage predates that of any of us now living here in their domain, and they deserve our respect, like any other community member.

Snapping Turtle Rescue

SEPTEMBER 1995 I recently had an experience that may be familiar to a number of people, who, in a fit of good samaritinism, may have chosen to stop and offer aid to wayward turtles on the road. The incident in question involved an eight-inch snapping turtle, an animal more reminiscent of an alligator with a shell on its back than the humble and friendly characters we've come to know from turtle cartoons.

I spied the reptile just as it began crawling onto the road. After pulling my truck safely over, I dutifully caught the animal and put it in the only container I had, which turned out to be a small plastic cage with a closing top (instead of the unorthodox animal containers I usually resort to, like kitchen Tupperware). The top of the cage was a snap-on affair with a small hinged lid built into it, and because the turtle fit snugly inside the little terrarium, I figured it would be secure until I could find a safe place to release it.

The snapping turtle was a little put out by its less-than-spacious quarters, and it immediately commenced to struggle mightily with the walls and top. I thought it was all in vain until I heard a resounding "pop" and saw the cage door flip open. I was confident the turtle was too large to fit through the small opening, and continued to drive along without thinking any more about the turtle's actions. However, amid strains of pent-up hisses, the highly vexed turtle soon succeeded in escaping through the cage door and hurriedly crawled out onto the passenger-side floorboard, while I motored along at highway speed.

I've had turtles loose on my truck floorboard before, including a couple of snapping turtles, and I don't really get concerned about them unless they make tracks toward my side of the vehicle. I fear they could wedge themselves in the awkward and dangerous spaces between the pedals and floor, which, inexplicably, is exactly where they always seem to want to go.

Being on a busy road, I couldn't do anything but hope the turtle would steer clear of the brake and gas pedals. And the turtle did stay away, choosing instead to crawl under the passenger-side seat. I was only slightly dismayed at its choice of places to go because I knew most of what was under there already: a coil of rope, a small net, maybe a pair of work gloves—nothing dangerous or of much consequence. The turtle clambered over all that and, after a brief pause to collect its turtle thoughts and reconsider its course of action, the determined animal proceeded to dig in and try to push its way through the tangle of spring steel supports and flimsy stuffing in the passenger seat.

I really had nowhere to pull off while all this was taking place, and the turtle's activities were proceeding at a very un-turtle-like pace. I caught fleeting glimpses as the seat cover mysteriously rose and fell, and each rise was punctuated with a muffled hiss of unquestionable exasperation. This, I must add, was soon followed by a particularly pungent aroma, unique, I believe, to agitated snapping turtles. In delicate conversation, the source of this perfume is called musk, which my truck quickly became doused with. The cab soon reeked of the unmistakable air of turtle.

By now, what really had me worried was not the effusive smell causing my eyes to nearly water, or the damage I suspected being done to the seat by the snapping turtle's rending claws, but rather how I was going to extract a very intractable turtle from among the seat springs without getting bitten.

But, as only turtle luck would have it, the angry snapper gave up its quest for freedom through the springs and cushion of the seat just as I pulled off the highway to more closely assess the situation. The turtle magically disentangled itself from the springs without any aid from me and proceeded to hunker down into the loose coil of rope with a final, prolonged sigh of indignation. As soon as I figured out which end was which, it was no effort lifting the poor beast out.

After looking the animal over, the only real sign that there had been any struggle at all on its part were a couple of small tufts of seat padding stuck in its front claws. Other than that, things appeared to be none the worse for wear (save for a not-so-subtle hint of musk emanating from beneath the seat). Fortunately, snapping turtle musk is short-lived and dissipates quickly; but that's about the least tenacious aspect I can think of to note about a snapping turtle's character.

A National Refuge for All

OCTOBER 2001 In honor of National Wildlife Refuge Week, I recently explored the salt marsh near my home and was delighted by the autumn congregation I found there.

A great blue heron, standing four feet tall amid the slender leaves of salt marsh cordgrass, was the first marsh inhabitant to reveal itself. The stately heron demonstrated its indignation when I came within about two hundred feet of it, by rising up on its large, steel-blue wings, and after two or three hoarse, croaking calls, flying a short distance up the creek before settling back down at the water's edge. I could sense it was eyeing me to make sure I didn't come too close, so I was careful not to follow a path in its direction.

Standing near the spot the heron had just left was another wading bird called a great egret, a smaller, pure white relative of the great blue heron. The egret seemed a little more comfortable with me being in the marsh and ignored my activities so long as I remained outside its personal space, which, I estimated, encompassed a radius of about a hundred feet. As I wandered the marsh creek, staying clear of the egret's space, I saw thousands of small fish, most of them finger-sized mullet, coursing through the shallows in dense schools. Mullet are silvery, cigar-shaped fish that feed on tiny plants and animals suspended in the water column or in the muddy marsh bottom. Some of the schooling mullet were so tightly packed that each time they moved to avoid a blue crab hunkered in the mud, they would leap from the water almost as a single entity. If the crab (or whatever else frightened the school) gave chase, the mullet would charge forward in a leapfrog manner, breaking the water's otherwise calm surface into a flurry of ripples.

In one particular bend in the creek, near where the great blue heron had been before my approach sent it away, I stood and watched school after school swim by as the tide flooded the marsh. Each time a school came to one spot in the bend, they would leap forward as though goosed by some unseen hand. Obviously, the heron and egret had picked up on this behavior and had staged themselves just past the bend, where the fish had to pass quite close to the shore. It was a riotous sight as the nervous mullet tried to get past one submerged gauntlet only to be set upon by a long-necked wading bird skulking above in the protective cover of the marsh grass.

I watched the egret's antics long enough to see it catch two small fish, and I decided to leave that stretch of the creek for the great blue heron to return to. As I followed the meandering creek, I heard the raucous cry of one of the marsh's most elusive avian residents. It was a clapper rail, a greenish-brown bird slightly larger than a city pigeon, but with longer legs, neck, and bill. The rail makes its living in the marsh feeding on fiddler crabs, worms, and small shrimps and fish it finds stranded in pools of water. Rails seldom leave the protective cover of the marsh grass, so I was thrilled when one pensively stepped into the open directly across the creek from me. The bird seemed to be oblivious of me and proceeded to investigate a small area of mud flat that the rising tide was starting to cover. The water must have been brimming with tasty little creatures because the rail darted its bill in determined dabs, pausing only long enough to swallow its captures, though I could not see what those were.

As quickly as it appeared, the rail silently disappeared back into the dense grass, and as it turned to go, I took its lead and headed home through the slowly rising saltwater. As I was leaving, I couldn't help thinking what a great attraction this "undesignated refuge" is, not just for October birds, but also for October bird watchers.

Grubbing Ibis

NOVEMBER 2004 Last week when I dropped off my sons at their high school, I spotted a pair of white ibises standing out on the school's baseball diamond. The following week, the number had grown to thirty-one birds, made up of about an equal mix of crisp, white-plumed adults and juveniles still sporting their drab, first-year charcoal feathers. White ibis are chicken-sized birds that inhabit our area in greatest numbers during the spring and summer, especially in the lower reaches of the Cape Fear River, where they find nesting habitat in the river's tree-covered Battery Island and their forage habitat in freshwater swamps and farm fields.

White ibis are specialized wading birds with fairly long legs that enable them to walk about in shallow water, probing the mud with their long, down-curved bill in search of live prey to feed themselves and their developing young. Very young ibises cannot process salt, so adults must forage in freshwater habitats for crayfish and other aquatic animals to feed their young offspring in the nest.

The ibises I recently observed were all old enough to handle whatever live foods they could catch and eat, wherever they could find it. White ibis are gregarious animals that roost, fly, and feed in groups. The pair I saw the first week may have served as scouts in search of good feeding grounds, who, having found it, led the much larger gathering the following week. After making my appointed school delivery, I pulled off the road near the ball field to watch the flock of birds, curious to know what they were feeding on. The pair of binoculars I'd placed in the glove box some time back provided me with a close-up view of the action.

Right away I saw one ibis grab something from the grass, but it bolted it down so quickly that I could only guess the treat had been a large grasshopper. I scanned the flock, hoping to see something else being captured, and in a moment I witnessed one bird probe its six-inch-long bill deep into the soil with jerky movements, as though trying to tweeze something from beneath. A second later, it extracted its bill, revealing a fat, two-inch-long morsel in the form of a beetle larva. Judging from the size of the beetle grub, coupled with their abundant numbers (evidenced by the success rates of the feeding birds), I speculated that the insects being consumed were members of the June-beetle clan. June beetles are large, generally shiny brown beetles that can often be seen on summer nights flying headlong into porch lights, or into windows illuminated by indoor lights.

Adult beetles feed very little, but their grub-like larvae can be a nuisance in lawns, especially those pampered with fertilizer and irrigation, because these places offer the best eats in the form of succulent roots. And herein lies an environmental irony for the ibis. Human residents have converted millions of acres of native habitats across the country into lawns that offer great sustenance to a wealth of so-called pest insects, including June-beetle larvae and another favorite insect of mine, the mole cricket.

White ibis, Eudocimus albus

We lay out a turf banquet for these and other insects, and when they come to dine, we poison them with untold varieties and volumes of pesticides. And in an ironic twist, suburban lawns across our nation receive upwards of three times the poundage per acre of toxic pesticides as the average American farm acre!

The white ibis, along with the American robin, the eastern bluebird, and dozens of other bird species, visit these same lawns to dine on the grass-eaters, and when these birds feed on poisoned fields—well, I have to wonder how long it will be before we find ourselves reading the second installment of Rachel Carson's *Silent Spring*.

Pygmy Rattler Rescue

NOVEMBER 2003 I came upon the snake by chance, as is almost always the case with any human-snake encounter. Sandy and I were driving along the gravel road that leads to our house when I noticed the familiar shape of a small serpent resting on the sun-heated gravel. I slid to a stop, which caught Sandy by surprise, but only for a moment, because such driving behavior has become common during our life together. I bailed out of the truck and heard her ask, "What is it?" as I hot-footed my way to the now alarmed serpent.

I replied that we had narrowly missed hitting a pygmy rattlesnake, and as I grabbed the snake hook and dip net from the truck, she asked, "What are you going to do with it?" Well, after all our years of marriage I almost felt I did not need to dignify the question with a response. But since she knew this was a venomous creature, I assured her that I would be very careful while removing it from the road, for its own safety as well as mine.

I then assured her that it would not be coming home, as is sometimes the case when one of us finds something in the road that might be of interest to the rest of the family— things like unusually large toads, or bigger-than-life beetles, or a snake with an especially attractive pattern. This particular snake would be released in a safer realm far away from any roads, not just because of its venomous bite, but also because pygmy rattlers are members of an elite group of protected venomous snakes in North Carolina. They are protected because they are rare due in part to habitat loss, and because the market for venomous pet snakes is growing.

Pygmy rattlesnakes are attractive by any snake measure, and some would even say they're cute, but only for their size. Most adult pygmies, as they are called in snake-keeping circles, seldom reach twenty-four inches; this one was nearly nineteen inches, making it large for its kind, and probably quite old as well. Pygmies make their living in our area in longleaf-pine forest. Their color varies from one region of their range to another—this one was reddish-brown, with dark gray blotches across its back, a perfect disguise for an animal relegated to a life on a forest floor. The pygmy rattler's head is small for a viper, but recognizably triangular, and a close look revealed the vertical, catlike pupils of the group, along with the small heat-detecting pits located between the eyes and the tiny nostrils at the tip of the snake's snout.

The pits give the rattlesnake, copperhead, and cottonmouth the collective name pit viper. They allow these specialized snakes to seek out and detect warm-blooded prey such as mice and rats. Pygmy rattlers grow large enough to eat full-grown mice, but they are as likely to eat small lizards and frogs, for which their heat-sensing pits may prove less valuable than their keen eyesight and sensitive tongue. Snakes flick their forked tongue in and out of their mouth to "taste" the world around them, and in this way they are able to locate food, water, and other essentials for life, including a mate. As with all pit vipers, the pygmy rattler gives birth to live young, usually in late summer and early autumn.

The pygmy that Sandy and I encountered was most likely taking advantage of the unusual warmth of a gravel road on this November day. No doubt it will prove to be one of the last snake days of the season, before the onset of winter, when this pygmy will be found sequestered beneath old logs and other similar shelters, safe from the chill. And speaking of safe: less than one minute from the time I bagged the little rattler, a large dump truck came barreling down our road, providing sober testimony that a road is no place for a snake, regardless of its venomous persuasion.

The Challenge of Flight

DECEMBER 2003 This week marks the hundredth anniversary of machine-powered human flight, but I just had an encounter with one flight-challenged individual whose ancestors were flying long before the word airplane meant anything.

It was a juvenile eastern brown pelican, and a rather morose-looking one at that. Brown pelicans are large waterbirds that nest in summer along the North American coast, especially on isolated sandy islands in the Cape Fear River but also on similar places north into the Chesapeake Bay and south to Texas and Mexico. Brown pelicans are plunge divers: they plunge headfirst into the water to capture small live fish with the aid of a large bill, equipped with an extensible throat pouch. The throat pouch serves as a baglike net to engulf the fish, along with more than a gallon of water that the pelican releases before swallowing its fishy prize.

I knew this was a juvenile bird because its head and neck were a drab gray color, rather than the crisp white-and-russet of adult birds. And this one was in a real fix, though it took me a couple minutes to figure out just what the problem was. At first it looked as though one wing was missing altogether, but after restraining it I could see that it was stranger than even that. I looked for fishing line that it might have gotten trussed up with—an all too common hazard for pelicans—but there was none. Then, as I worked my hands over its back and wings, it became evident what had happened; but as I realized the problem, I became flustered trying to figure out how to fix it.

The bird's right wing had somehow become tangled under and around its left one, almost like a twist tie. As soon as I realized this, I started to worry that an attempt to untangle the wings might lead to a broken wing bone or dislocated joint. It might help to picture this bird's plight by understanding what a bird's wings really are. Wings are essentially arms, containing humerus bones that attach to shoulder girdles, not unlike ours. Attached to the humerus bone at the elbow are the radius and ulna bones, the longest wing bones. At the tip of the bird's wing (or arm if you prefer) is an odd-looking fusion of digits and wrist bones. The pelican's wingspan is more than seven feet from tip to tip, but much of that length is made up of primary feathers that extend well beyond the tip of the bird's actual wing bone.

I studied the matter anxiously for a while before trying to return the displaced wing back to its rightful place. After some delicate coaxing, I was able to free the tip end of the right wing—the radius and ulna part—from under the humerus portion of the left wing. Then, with a gut-wrenching twist, I was able to untangle the remaining limb parts, and the pelican immediately stretched its wings, but only once, as it must have been terribly uncomfortable after being in that predicament.

How it came to be that way I may never know, but I would

guess it happened while diving into the water. When brown pelicans dive into the water, they extend their wings behind them, and I suppose this one somehow got twisted yoga-fashion when it retracted its wings into the folded position. It had been like this long enough to grow thin from lack of food.

I placed the hungry bird in a large box and called on two wonderful friends of injured wildlife to help rehabilitate the animal so it could try its luck at life in its native environment once again. Jean in Hampstead provided fresh frozen fish, and our falconer friend Mike, also in Hampstead, took possession of the bird to provide it with a spacious flight cage where it could eat and mend its sore muscles before being released.

With the celebration of human flight underway on the Outer Banks of North Carolina, I can't help but think about all the other earthlings that took flight before us, including the usually graceful eastern brown pelican. The Wright Brothers' journey into the air was fraught with great challenges, and the pioneer aviators no doubt had help from friends in the process, kind of like this temporarily flight-challenged pelican.

Solstice Owls

December 1999 Recently Sandy and I sat watching our winter-solstice campfire burn down to glowing embers, when a sound came suddenly to our ears: the haunting *hoot-hoot* call of a great horned owl. The call was muted by distance and trees, but its source was obvious, and we could tell it was located out over the upper reaches of Bradley Creek, less than a quarter mile from where we sat huddled near the retiring fire.

The great horned owl is our area's largest resident owl. Adults stand nearly a foot-and-a-half tall and carry themselves silently on wings that span four feet across. Horned owls get their name from the pair of curious feather tufts above their eyes that the owl raises and lowers much like a cat would do its ears. The owl's plumage is made of soft feathers in various shades of russet, brown, tan, and black. The mixture of colors helps the owl blend into the woodland background where it spends the day sleeping. The only flaw in its camouflage is a pair of piercing yellow eyes that stare straight forward when the bird looks at something.

Owls are nocturnal hunters that depend on noiseless stealth so that their rodent prey won't hear their approaching wingbeats. Owls silence their flight with specialized flight feathers that are soft and pliable and thus make little sound when swept through the air. In contrast to its quiet movements, the great horned owl's call is loud and deep, a resonant series of four to six monotone *hoot-hoot*s. The calls this time of year serve as auditory boundary markers for other owls, and they also help owl pairs keep tabs on one another's location. While it may seem early for most birds to think about nest making, it's not so for the horned owl, some of whom may already be sitting on eggs.

As we listened to the song of the great horned owl, another horned owl called from some distance behind us, which placed us directly between two calling owls. The two traded hoots for a few minutes, and with each alternate refrain, it seemed like the birds drew closer to where Sandy and I sat, spellbound, almost holding our breaths so as not to miss the next call. Then, as suddenly as the first two birds had started calling, there came the earnest, four part *hoot-hoot, hoot-hoot* call of a third owl. The location of the new bird formed a triangle of owls around the two of us, but only briefly. Very quickly after the third owl joined the singsong, all three birds fell silent. We also sat in excited silence, waiting, almost expecting to hear one of the birds calling from a perch above our heads, but the trio remained quiet.

Though the moon was shrouded by heavy clouds, it was nonetheless very bright outside. The black silhouettes of large, solitary pine and hardwood trees stood out clearly around the marsh. These are the same trees the owls use as their travel corridors—corridors that intersect our lawns, neighborhoods, roads, and rivers, composed of trees that delineate the home range of individual owls, or pairs of owls.

While ours is a world carved up by artificial easements and property lines, the owl's world is composed of open space punctuated by trees: two residents in the same community bounded by what almost seem to be different realities, one illuminated by day and one shrouded by night.

I pondered for a time the many happenings that go on outside our doors on any given night that I fail to observe, including the wandering travels and melodic hoots of these great horned owls. But a sudden pop from a smoldering piece of cedar erased my brief regrets, and quickly reminded me that these things are observable to those who happen to be sitting quietly outside, on a wintry night, watching a campfire fall silent.

A Loon in Plight

DECEMBER 2003 About two weeks ago, I received a call regarding an injured bird sitting on the top level of a parking deck at the beach.

I reached the parking deck just as a rain cloud started to unleash its store, and I drove up the ramps and around the decks until I found the bird where I was told it would be: sitting in a corner of the parking deck. It was a species of bird known as the common loon, a diving waterbird that spends the breeding season amid freshwater lakes in more northern climates, including much of Canada. In winter, common loons migrate to the southeastern coastline to escape ice that would otherwise prevent them from capturing their fishy prey.

The common loon is a streamlined, duck-sized diving bird that swims along the surface of placid waters with the aid of large, webbed feet. An adept predator, the loon trains its eyes to the water beneath it, searching for the glinting shimmer of a small fish to eat. In fact, loons are so keenly adapted to a life in and on water that they have all but lost the ability to move on land without great difficulty. Loons' legs are set far back on the body in order to maximize paddling propulsion, which makes paddling easier, but walking near impossible—imagine using a boat's propeller to cross a grassy field. In order to gain flight, a loon must have a large open area of water to get a running start, using its webbed feet to patter along the surface as it pumps its wings, trying to get airborne.

This is why we sometimes find loons in unorthodox places such as parking lots, streets, and open beaches. When grounded, due to harsh weather or having mistakenly landed in a puddle over concrete in search of a larger body of water, the common loon is essentially stranded, because it does not have the water it needs to help it gain any forward lift. This is what I imagine happened to the loon on the parking deck—it just landed in the wrong place.

I pulled up to within a car's length of the bird, knowing it could not run or fly away. When I stepped out from behind the vehicle's door with a blanket in hand to wrap the bird in, what had been a passive, helpless-looking creature transformed into a defensive, saber-wielding terror with bright, piercing eyes. (Well, not really, but if it could have envisioned itself as anything other than a grounded loon, I should think it fancied itself a terror.)

I was taken aback by the bird's change of demeanor as it uttered a mournful wail that loons usually reserve for their breeding grounds. Then, as suddenly as it had called out, the bird lunged toward me in a pathetic manner that looked more like it had tripped on a step than attempted an attack. Its aggressive forward movement spanned a foot and a half before the bird halted to regroup itself. I dropped the blanket on the poor beast and restrained its business end, namely, the sharply pointed bill.

There was blood on its breast feathers, but a quick examination revealed that the blood was actually coming from its feet, which it had been resting on when I pulled up. The tender skin of its toes had abraded on the concrete, and the wounds bled profusely. Everything else about the bird appeared fine, so I packed it in a box and drove to a nearby tidal creek, where I unceremoniously released it into the water. The instant it hit the water, the loon was back in its element and dove immediately, resurfacing only after having put some thirty feet between us. It looked back for a moment, then dove again and did not resurface until it was well over a hundred feet away.

This bird would be fine so long as it stayed in the water. But, as happens every year, loons like this one find themselves stranded in the wrong place. And while some may indeed be injured from car strikes, entanglement in fishing line, or natural causes, I have discovered that many stranded loons just need to be led back to the water where they belong.

The Individuality of Ponds

FEBRUARY 1999 I recently visited a wonderful tract of land in New Hanover County that contains a relic stretch of sandhills habitat harboring a diverse collection of isolated ponds.

I used to worry about the shortage of water in the basins of the tract's two largest ponds, but this year they're very near their maximum holding capacity. However, more significant in my mind is the fact that, for the first time since I have been watching this particular area, there are now three more sites filled with water. All three are very small. Two are circular in shape, less than twenty feet across, and they hold about three feet of water in the middle. The third pond is more elongate, about forty feet long and fifteen feet wide, with a maximum depth of two to three feet. Around this latter pond are several shrubs, including a rare species of Litsea called pondspice that is found only in southeastern North America.

I had seen water in the elongate pond and in one of the round ponds after Hurricane Fran in 1996 and during the 1997 El Niño rainy season. During this period, each contained a complement of frog and toad tadpoles and some aquatic invertebrates, including dragonflies, damselflies, and tiny crustaceans: copepods, daphnia, and seed shrimp. The other round pond had been dry since I first started watching it several years before, so it was a surprise to see it holding water.

The significance of the water struck me as I looked into the tea-colored water and saw hundreds of inch-long fairy shrimp swimming gracefully beneath the surface. Fairy shrimp are ephemeral pool inhabitants, which means they live in pools that dry up during the summer. Their salt-water cousins, called brine shrimp, have been depicted in comic-book advertisements as "Sea Monkeys," a less-than-glamorous name for a dainty and elegant creature. Since this particular pond was filled for the first time in at least five years, the fairy shrimp I saw sculling blithely in its water had to have hatched from eggs that were laid by a generation that lived that many years ago. Through the intervening years, the shrimp rested as dormant eggs in the soil at the bottom of this pond, waiting for rains to come and fill their nursery and allow them to hatch and carry on a legacy that goes back hundreds, if not thousands, of years.

There were no predatory insects in this particular pond, but the other two ponds, which have had water in them in recent years, both contained predatory dragonflies and water tiger beetle larvae, proof that the water they held was not especially new. The fairy shrimp in these ponds hatched from eggs that were laid only a year or two ago, by adults I remember watching and marveling over during that time.

This study in pond diversity becomes all the more intriguing when you look at all five ponds at once and see just how different they are from one another while being in such close proximity. The ponds have been around for probably

the same amount of time—maybe a couple of centuries—
and through it all they've survived a civil war, the pine-tar
era, countless natural forest fires, and, lastly, logging. These
diminutive ponds and their collections of plants and animals
held on. The trials and tribulations their unique sandhills
community has imposed on them shaped and molded each
pond into an entity in itself.

In the relatively short time that I have been able to spend
with them, I have come to know each pond as an individual,
with attributes no other pond shares. Like snowflakes that
have no match, these five ponds have no equals, which makes
them all the more enjoyable—and enlightening—to explore,
and therefore all the more imperative to protect.

Resourceful White Ibis

APRIL 2004 I recently had the privilege of exploring some of the dredge islands located in the middle of the Cape Fear River, not far from where it empties into the ocean. The islands were created as a result of river-dredging activities over past decades, and most are rather small, ranging from just a few acres (in the case of Ferry Slip Island) to Battery Island, which encompasses over one hundred acres just offshore from Southport.

Many of the river's dredge islands serve as winter roosting habitat and summer nesting habitat to a great wealth of birdlife because they are essentially inaccessible to land-bound predators such as raccoons and cats. As part of the Audubon Society's Coastal Sanctuary system, many of these islands are managed to provide nesting habitat for colonial waterbirds, including white ibis, eastern brown pelicans, various herons and egrets, and several other species. A few weeks ago I was visiting Battery Island to help get it ready for the annual spring arrival of thousands of nest-building wading birds, including more than 14,000 pairs of nesting white ibis—representing almost ten percent of all the nesting individuals of this species in North America.

At first glance, white ibis resemble small egrets, but the ibis has a longer, down-curved bill that tapers to a blunt tip, where the egret's bill is straight and pointed. Ibises have been using Battery Island as a nesting sight for decades, though not in the impressive numbers seen in recent years. The increase in their population is partly due to its being predator-free, but more important, the island contains a sizable stand of large, suitable nest trees, including yaupon and red cedar. Battery Island is also located in close proximity to good forage habitat—the freshwater swamps and marshes of Brunswick, Columbus, New Hanover, and Pender Counties. These freshwater habitats are key elements in the life history of the ibis, because young ibises cannot eat the salty foods, such as fiddler crabs, found in salt marshes. Ibis parents must instead fly to nearby freshwater habitats to gather low-salt crayfish and insects to feed their hungry offspring.

White ibises build stick nests in the island's trees, and as I looked around the branches, I saw signs of nests from previous years, all in varying degrees of dilapidation. The old nests will become more dilapidated once this year's flocks arrive and begin to recycle them for construction materials. Sticks are a premium commodity to nest-building ibis on a relatively small island with a finite supply of trees. In coming days, hundreds and then thousands of white ibises will scour the ground and trees for every stick they can find, remove, or carry, from tiny twigs to lanky branches. Any manageable stick will do, including those that are part of another bird's nest. Ibis are not beneath thievery when it comes to such resources.

To help expand the existing forest, small trees are planted on the island by Audubon staff every year, with help from Cape Fear Garden Club volunteers. Their hope is for the small trees to one day grow large enough to become nesting habitat for future ibis. However, sticks are so valuable to the island's nest-building ibises that in an ironic twist of bird conservation, wire-screen cages must be built around small yaupon holly and red cedar plants, to prevent marauding ibis from stripping the small trees before they've grown.

I can't help but ponder the irony of having to protect these future ibis nesting trees from today's nesting birds. The ibises' inability to understand the need to conserve valuable, finite resources that their future generations will need is an interesting parallel to the seeming inability of our own species to understand the same. I say this in context to our current use of fossil fuels, and what our actions today may mean for our own future generations.

As I see it, the big difference between people and ibis is, we have the wherewithal to avoid predictable resource depletions. Birds do not. I think we can learn a conservation lesson from the ibis: that stripping finite resources to satisfy what today's generation *wants* may not be in the best interest of our future generations, and the things they will *need*.

Alligator Surprise

MAY 1994 As a teacher and naturalist, I spend a lot of time talking about where and how to watch wildlife, from algae-feeding aquatic mosquito larvae to carrion-eating vultures. Of course, when demonstrating various wildlife-watching techniques, I am obligated to recite some precautions relative to field studies. So it came as no small embarrassment one day, as I led a freshwater pond workshop for a group of teaching fellows, that one of the pond's residents caught me off guard and completely by surprise.

The workshop participants had been involved in various outdoor teaching experiences for the previous few days, and my pond activity with them was to be the workshop's last field experience. I took the group to a well-vegetated pond in south New Hanover County, not far from the Cape Fear River. I knew the pond contained a lot of small fishes and aquatic insects, and a nice mix of basking turtles. After my lengthy discourse on pond ecology, freshwater collecting techniques, and pond-study safety, the group divided into teams and went about their appointed task—collecting interesting plants and animals with dip nets that we could look at and identify in shallow trays.

Of course, I was having as much fun as the students were, and when one of the other instructors spotted a small alligator, I seized the opportunity to demonstrate the acoustical acuity of this familiar reptile. Alligators rely on their keen hearing to identify the calls of other gators or the movements of animals in water. The alligator measured some five to six feet in length, resting quietly at the surface about thirty feet from where we stood at the pond's edge. I asked the group to remain still while I proceeded to the water's edge, which was grown over with thick grasses and lance-shaped pickerelweed leaves. Squatting down in the grass, I began imitating, as best I could, the distress call of a hatchling alligator, which sounds a little like a throaty peep. At the same time, I gently patted the water's surface, making a subtle splashing sound as though produced by a struggling small animal. Everyone's eyes were glued to the small alligator, as it first turned its gaze toward me and then slowly started to cruise in my direction. At least I thought the students were looking at the inquisitive gator.

Having "charmed" the gator to approach me, I turned to the group to say something, and instantly a powerful and loud splash erupted not five feet away from where I squatted. The unexpected commotion was caused by a second gator that, unobserved by me, had been slowly lurking its way in my direction. I jumped up and backed away from the water's edge, jokingly explaining that I did not wish to block anyone's view of this second animal. Then, a little embarrassed, I took the opportunity to point out that a careful advance survey of any area to be explored is a prerequisite to a safe field trip.

It turned out that the entire group saw the second gator the whole while, and they all assumed I had seen it too.

Everyone, including myself, got a good laugh from the experience, albeit at my expense. But that close call with a gator was nothing compared to what happened during my demonstration of the sensory abilities of another aquatic denizen called the backswimmer.

Backswimmers are half-inch-long, oval-shaped black bugs that swim upside down, usually just below the water's surface. They propel themselves through the water with a pair of oarlike elongate hind limbs. Backswimmers are predators that specialize in catching mosquito larvae and other small prey. Tiny sensory hairs on their body detect vibrations on the water's surface, as when a fly or other tiny animal falls in. When the backswimmer feels the vibrations, it quickly swoops in, and with unerring precision, grasps the victim with its four short front legs, delivering a paralyzing bite with its sharp, piercing mouth.

And that's how it happened to me when I was demonstrating the struggling efforts of a fly in water. My painful mistake came when I looked up at my audience while belaboring the backswimmer's cunning ability. The backswimmer deftly grasped my finger and delivered a swift, piercing bite that prompted me to jerk my hand from the jar with an utterance usually reserved for mishaps with a hammer. I could have easily avoided the bite had I just removed my finger from the water while my attention was elsewhere. But I didn't, which may be just as well, for the experience will no doubt serve as a lasting reminder for the teachers-to-be—that when interacting with wildlife, regardless of size, vigilant attention to safety is a must.

A Loggerhead's Last Saga

MAY 1996 Last week I had the grim occasion to witness the passing of an old resident of southeastern North Carolina. Her age can only be speculated, though I figure somewhere between thirty and sixty years. Her life was spent at sea, and her infrequent visits to land were confined to narrow stretches of sandy beach along the coast. Her stays there lasted a mere few hours. All the intervening hours, day and night, were spent plying the vast expanse that is the Atlantic Ocean.

I came to know this remarkable individual by unfortunate chance; it seems that during her last foray onto dry land, she became the unwitting target of some large vehicle.

In life, she was a 250-pound, 42-inch-long loggerhead seaturtle, and her fateful, final act was one of propagation, an arduous process fraught with too many dangers for one animal to deserve.

Loggerheads propagate by following an age-old formula that begins with a male and female mating at sea not far from shore. The male internally fertilizes the female's eggs, about a hundred at a time, and a short week or two later, the female, as bulging as a turtle can get, swims to shore, preferably on a dark stretch. Then she crawls up the beach above the high tide line, and that is where she begins nest building. Using her hind flippers as shovels, the laboring turtle scoops a cavity less than a foot across and about eighteen inches deep, or until she is satisfied the sand nest will hold all her eggs. Once the nest is complete she deposits her clutch of eggs, covers the nest with sand, turns back toward the sea, and crawls home to the water. The nest is on its own for the two months it takes the eggs to develop.

The turtle I met last week had either just finished, or was just finishing, this ritual when her life came to a crushing halt. I mean that literally. By our best reckoning based on physical evidence on the beach, the female turtle was run over, most likely by a reckless beach vehicle. Her top shell, the carapace, was completely crushed when beach walkers found her, but she tenaciously clung to life. Turtle stranding network members were notified and quickly responded to the scene. Realizing the turtle could not go back safely to the water, the members collected her into a transport and carried her to the North Carolina Aquarium, which is where I met her.

I feel a little guilty focusing on this turtle's untimely end, because I've seen it dozens of times before with equally old and wizened turtles—box turtles mostly, along with sliders and snapping turtles. These smaller turtles, injured and killed on our highways by the thousands, deserve the same recognition we too often reserve only for the mighty seaturtles. The fact that this large animal, brought to us moments before expiring, happened to be a loggerhead seaturtle, is no reason to feel more compassionate than we would for any other species of turtle suffering the same fate. It's easy to say that, but standing at her side, holding her massive front flipper as she breathed her last, I have to admit it was a little different than watching a pond turtle undergo the same throes.

What truly moved me about this individual turtle was what she did with her last spark of life. In spite of her crushed shell and back, she continued the motions of nest building with her hind flippers. The movements were not uncontrolled or out of panic or despair; she clearly made controlled movements with her hind feet as though digging a nest. This turtle was on a mission, and her selfless act of determination was as heroic an effort as any wild animal can make. And it proved to me that nature's treasures will try to persevere in spite of all adversity.

3

Beyond All That

Life and Death in a Pond Drop

APRIL 1992 We tend to assume that humans are the best parents in the animal kingdom, and there's no doubt that we expend vast resources and use much of our intelligence to raise our offspring. But I've found that some of the lower forms of life are also conscientious parents.

Take daphnia for example, the "water flea" as they are often called. Adult daphnia are no bigger than a typewritten lowercase "o", and though they are related to crabs and shrimps, they more closely resemble a tiny plant seed with hair-thin legs and jointed antennae. Daphnia are common in small ponds and ditches, especially those where there are no fish to eat them. They are short-lived animals that must mature quickly and produce viable offspring before the water they live in dries away. As proof of their rapid life cycle, I have already found mature, pregnant daphnia in small ponds that have been filled with water for only a couple of weeks.

One really interesting trait of these little animals is that while rains are abundant and their ponds brimming, daphnia give birth to fully developed live offspring—exact miniature replicas of the adult. But once the rains stop and their pond starts to dry, the female daphnia stop giving birth to live young and produce instead a dozen or so dark gray, hard-shelled eggs that, after being ejected, settle to the bottom and stay dormant and unhatched until the next rainy season refills the pond, even if that takes several years. Under a hand lens, a rainy-season pregnant daphnia looks as though she is packed with two to five miniature replicas of herself. These are her developing babies, and she will carry them to full term. Obviously there must be benefits to this reproductive strategy, since daphnia have been around for a very long time, but I have found some pretty strange drawbacks to it as well. The most memorable of these was the time I caught a female daphnia ready to give birth to her live offspring. Close scrutiny revealed she was carrying a hitchhiking hydra on her back, a freshwater pond counterpart of an ocean's sea anemone. The translucent-white hydra possesses a number of long tentacles covered with stinging cells, which are used to capture live prey, including tiny copepods and daphnia.

As luck would have it, I had deposited the daphnia in a microscope slide, which I then placed in a slide projector so I could enlarge the animal's image on a white wall and allow a camera crew from a local television station to collect footage of small pond inhabitants for a news story. As I examined the daphnia, somewhat amazed that it had its arch-enemy anchored to its back, it began to give birth. The first baby daphnia to emerge was instantly snared by the hydra's stinging tentacles and devoured. In a matter of moments, two more daphnia were born without incident. I doubt this is a common phenomenon. In fact I am certain it is quite rare, but nonetheless, the episode has me wondering if hydra are somehow able to seek out pregnant daphnia to take advantage of this bounty.

Not only was I fortunate to have witnessed this possibly once-in-a-lifetime natural event projected on my wall, but so were the two people standing with me, their camera at the ready. The equipment was positioned and ready to roll, but because we were all so engrossed in what was transpiring on the wall, none of us had the foresight to turn the camera on. You can imagine the chagrined looks on our faces as that realization set in. Trying to be philosophical about it now, I suppose it was meant not to be captured on film, if only to assure that I will keep a sharp eye out for other wonders of nature to be found, literally, in every drop of water.

Mosquitoes: What Are They Good For?

APRIL 1989 Warm spring and summer evenings bring a variety of nighttime song. Among the most familiar (and often annoying) is the shrill whine of tiny wings produced by mosquitoes. Somewhere around the fourth or fifth unsuccessful slap, a question inevitably arises: What are mosquitoes good for anyway?

To answer this question, we must begin where the life of a mosquito begins: as an egg in water. A female mosquito that bites and draws blood does so to nourish the many developing eggs she carries inside her. She lays these eggs on the surface of virtually any water source, from ponds and ditches to old cans and tires holding rainwater. In fact, an old tire filled with just a little bit of water can support more than a hundred mosquito larvae at any given time.

The eggs hatch in a few days and the larvae, known as wrigglers, begin feeding on microscopic plants and detritus. Throughout their development and growth, the mosquito larvae must contend with the threat of becoming a meal for a host of aquatic predators, including dragonflies. As with the mosquito, the beneficial dragonfly also begins its life in water, and its aquatic larvae feed heavily on an assortment of animals, including mosquito larvae. Diving beetles, salamander larvae, and almost any small fish also feed on the abundant mosquito larvae; one fish in particular is so well adapted to feeding on mosquito larvae that it has been given the name mosquitofish. This inch-and-a-half-long fish thrives in backwaters and nearly stagnant ditches, areas that can breed mosquitoes by the hundreds of thousands. This fish is so effective at controlling mosquitoes that it has been introduced in some areas as a substitute for pesticides.

The consumption of one animal by another is, in a sense, an exchange of energy. The energy from mosquito larvae is transferred to dragonfly larvae and mosquito fish. They in turn are eaten by larger aquatic predators, including other fishes, turtles, and frogs.

Still larger predators, including herons, osprey, and even humans, consume the turtles, fish, and frogs. The largemouth bass that many of us enjoy catching and eating can only grow large because it has derived energy through a chain of events beginning with, and often based on, a healthy mosquito population. But what about the adult mosquitoes? Who eats them? You may not like the sight of a small, furry bat, but they relish the sight, or sound, of a swarm of mosquitoes. And adult dragonflies can consume fifty to one hundred mosquitoes every day of their one- to two-week adult life. Purple martins, contrary to popular belief, do not eat mosquitoes; they prefer larger prey, like dragonflies, deerflies, and horseflies. However, barn swallows and chimney swifts, smaller relatives of the martin, do eat mosquitoes.

One of the least-known benefits of the mosquito is its ability to pollinate very small flowers that larger insects like bees and butterflies can't. Another thing many people do not know about this unsung hero is that only female mosquitoes bite. Male mosquitoes don't have the stabbing mouthpart needed to draw blood. Male mosquitoes, and most females for that matter, get their nourishment from flower nectar.

So, before we wish for the extinction of the mosquito, let's be sure we understand the long-term impact that mosquito extinction, however unlikely it may be, would have on our future. For a wheel to spin correctly, it must first have a full complement of spokes—and this round world needs all the spokes it can keep.

A World at Fault

APRIL 1989 The spectacular oil spill in Prince William Sound, Alaska, has captured our attention for many days. It promises to be, as Environmental Protection Agency director William Reilly has said, "a major environmental catastrophe."

But the matter of the *Exxon Valdez* is more than that. It has a lot to teach us about how we treat the environment and how we react to the despoiling of it. If only we would listen.

Once the news broke, attention quickly turned toward arresting the ship's captain, who was said to have been drunk below deck when the tanker strayed from the center of a ten-mile-wide shipping channel and twice struck rocks before running hard aground and spilling eleven million gallons of oil.

It certainly sounds like his fault. But it's my fault, too. And I don't make that admission lightly. I knew, along with thousands of other people, that given the extensive development of oil fields in a place as hostile and remote to shipping as Alaska, that a spill would be inevitable. We knew it because the oil industry admitted it, albeit behind a smokescreen of statistics.

I, along with millions of others on the first Earth Day, in 1970, stood up and demanded that we take stock and reverse the wholesale disregard of our environment. I, along with millions of others, gave up too easily after the battle to prevent the Trans-Alaska pipeline was lost.

I reject the absolution given us by the administration that claims there's just not a whole lot you can do to prevent something like this. Those of us who were environmentalists in 1970 knew that the pipeline would terminate at a sound where the fishery is worth hundreds of millions of dollars, where glacier calves abound in the shipping channel, and where a spill would be difficult to contain and catastrophic if it weren't.

We should've made sure that alcohol consumption on the job did not become acceptable, as it apparently had been, among the crews of supertankers. We should have fought for double-hulled tankers to reduce the chance of just such a spill as this one, and we should have demanded that smaller compartments be required to reduce the magnitude of any spill should those measures fail. We should have pushed through a legal requirement that containment equipment be readily available in every place that tankers operate in close quarters with sensitive wildlife habitat.

But with the exception of a few souls crying in the wilderness, most of us went on about our business. Maybe, we let ourselves think, the oilmen are right. Maybe it will happen someday when we don't have to worry about it. But of course, the problems didn't go away. We did.

If we still felt the same passion for our planet as we did on Earth Day 1970, a lot of us would admit that. We would admit that we as a nation should not have been so eager to sink oil wells in the Alaska wilderness just so we could drive to the store to buy a single item of convenience, or drive across the street to avoid putting on a raincoat. On the first Earth Day, a lot of us never imagined that nineteen years later we ourselves would be sitting in cars and burning gas while waiting in line for a hamburger packed in a Styrofoam box.

It's become all too easy to say it is someone else's responsibility to assure a clean and healthy environment for our grandchildren. It's easy to blame the oil industry for not thinking ahead, for not realizing that the cost of preventing pollution pales in significance to the cost of cleaning it up. But the environmentalists who clamored for industry to assume its environmental responsibility should have remained vigilant, and should have helped industry to become responsible. I'm one of them.

The wreck of the *Exxon Valdez* is not just the messy handiwork of a drunken sailor, nor of a corporation obsessed with profit. It is a symbol of how we are failing at the most important issue of our time: treating the failing health of the truly unique planet that we're fated to travel upon. War, famine, drugs, disease, drought, global warming, ozone depletion—these are symptoms of larger issues of global environmental health.

Earth Day took place many years ago, this month. I suppose we've learned a lot since then, but we seem to have forgotten a lot, too.

Loggerhead Lights

JUNE 2000 The loggerhead is North Carolina's most common species of nesting seaturtle, and June is one of the most important months for these animals to nest, especially during full moons. The reason loggerheads pick full moons to nest by is not fully understood, nor is much else of their behavior.

One possibility is that the moon's light helps navigate and orient the adult turtle or her young when they hatch out after their two-month incubation. When the one-inch-high hatchlings pop up onto the sand surface, they have a very limited view of their surroundings; even a small shell can block a tiny turtle's view of the ocean. But the turtles are somehow able to find their way even in the dark of night. And here's where the moon may come in.

Moonlight reflecting off the ocean's surface forms a bright horizon. Seaturtle hatchlings can orient on the brighter horizon and march toward it, all the way to the water. Does this mean the adult turtles use the dark horizon to orient on land, where they must lay their eggs? That may be a subject for up and coming seaturtle researchers to try to solve, though it is a question worth some thought today by those of us who have beachfront property.

One particularly fine June night, as my family and I walked a stretch of local beach, watching the waxing moon rise up over the ocean, we were amazed at the profusion of lights glaring up and down the shoreline, casting a pretty obnoxious urban glow on what should otherwise have been a romantically moonlit North Carolina beach. I understand the need for security lighting in certain places, but most of the light pollution on the beach that night was actually coming from ornamental floodlights, not security bulbs.

Research has shown that light pollution on beaches can disorient and confuse seaturtles. The excess light, and the human activity it illuminates, may discourage adult female turtles from nesting on a particular beach. And on beaches where turtles do nest, when the hatchlings erupt onto the sand surface, they are easily drawn toward the brightest light around, be it streetlight, floodlight, or moonlight. Florida has led the way in implementing guidelines for light pollution reduction, and so far that state's efforts have paid off with good seaturtle nesting numbers, as well as the bonus of tourism along beaches that have turtle-watch programs.

Seaturtles are plagued with peril from the moment they start out as eggs in sand. Nests may be raided by raccoons and other predators, and when the hatchlings emerge from the nest, they are set upon by gulls all day and ghost crabs all night. Once the two-inch-long turtles enter the water, they're vulnerable to fish, including bluefish, mackerel, and sharks. If they survive the arduous swim to the safety of sargassum seaweed rafts floating forty-plus miles from shore, the turtles may grow to a venerable age of thirty to seventy years and weigh more than four hundred pounds. But even at that age and size, the turtles are not safe. Collisions with fast boats and entanglement in gill and trawl nets still take a heavy toll on seaturtles oceanwide.

Light pollution on beaches doesn't just disorient and confuse seaturtles, but also other light-sensitive animals, including many kinds of birds, especially during their annual migration flights that carry them along our coasts.

I realize ordinances may require lighting in certain places, but those rules are generally put in place with little thought to the impact it may have on the rest of our community, including neighbors, seaturtles, and other wildlife.

Seaturtles play valuable roles in the ocean that we may never fully understand. But in order to protect future generations of seaturtles for the next generations of marine researchers to study years from now, we will have to make an effort today to assure the greatest possible chance that seaturtles will be around for them to study. To that end, with all the other perils seaturtles and other beleaguered wildlife must face, is it really too much to ask: Please, turn out the lights.

Snapping Turtle Unveiled

JUNE 1988 The common snapping turtle that inhabits our ponds, streams, and lakes performs a service that has been misunderstood for many years. Considered by many a useless predator of game fish and ducks, this often maligned turtle actually fills an important niche in the aquatic environment.

A hatchling snapping turtle emerges from its round, leathery eggshell in early fall after a two-month incubation in a ten-inch-deep nest that the mother snapper has dug, usually not far from water. The hatchlings may be vulnerable to winter cold, so they often remain in their nest until the following spring. When the two-inch-long hatchling snapping turtle appears on the pond scene, it is easily identified by its rough black shell and characteristically long neck and tail—a tail that is longer than the youngster's own shell. Upon reaching the water, the vulnerable hatchling seeks the safety of the pond bottom and spends its first few years searching the pond weeds for small aquatic insects, crayfish, tadpoles, and fishes to eat.

By its fifth year, the snapping turtle's shell measures nearly seven inches long, and its stout, scaly, dragonlike tail is an impressive four inches long. When the turtle is fully grown, its shell may measure eighteen inches and its weight may exceed forty pounds. At this size, the snapping turtle's name befits it, and careless handling by even well-intentioned people can result in a nasty bite.

The adult snapping turtle is an opportunistic feeder that spends most of its time on or near the pond bottom. Though a fairly fast swimmer, the bulky snapper cannot hope to chase down and capture a healthy fish like a bass or sunfish; instead, the snapper, with its cryptic, rocklike appearance, lurks on the pond bottom, relying on concealment and ambush.

Of course, the reputation of this turtle is that of a duck-eater. And while it is true that a large snapper will take a small duck that swims by, the ducks and snappers occupy different zones in the pond, and this type of encounter is one of chance that the turtle cannot depend on as a steady source of food. So the snapping turtle has, out of need, developed a preference for food that cannot escape so easily, including sickly and already dead animals near the pond bottom. This is where the snapper's true worth becomes evident: it consumes diseased animals that might otherwise threaten healthy populations, and it removes carrion that would otherwise putrefy and pollute the water.

By performing these tasks, the common snapping turtle can be seen as it truly is—a natural sanitation engineer for the pond. But snappers are more than just living garbage cans. While they do remove some healthy animals, their predatory behavior helps hone the gene pool of pond animals that need to be wary, including the ducks. So, in the big scheme of life in a pond, the snapping turtle, like a lion out on an African plain, helps keep populations of prey animals sharp and healthy.

An Endangered Species Conundrum

JULY 1994 For almost three years now, I've been involved in a race against time and development, trying to keep one little-known and very interesting southeastern North Carolina animal off the infamous Endangered Species Act list. It's a rare species of snail, known among malacologists as *Planorbella magnifica*, the magnificent rams-horn snail. Southeastern North Carolina has several other species of rams-horn snail, including the abundantly common marsh rams-horn. The rams-horn group is so named by the way their shell spirals. Rather than spiraling out into a pointed cone, the rams-horn snail spirals outward on a single plane, looking somewhat like a small toy wheel. The common marsh rams-horn can be found around here in just about any ditch, pond, or lake, and in some habitats their numbers can be counted in the hundreds per cubic foot.

Rams-horn snails are pulmonate—they possess a saclike internal organ that functions somewhat like a lung. Pulmonate snails can breathe underwater, but they can come to the surface to get a good breath of oxygen from the air if the water becomes anoxic (oxygen-poor, as from pollution or other causes).

The marsh rams-horn and magnificent rams-horn look casually similar when they're newly hatched, but as they grow, the marsh snail remains compressed, while the shell of *magnifica* (as I like to call it) flares out and becomes almost ball-shaped.

Both species of snail lay eggs in flat, gelatinous masses, usually on submerged plants and other objects. I've found marsh snail eggs on everything in the water from tree trunks to trash. But there's something noteworthy about the egg-laying strategy of *magnifica*: almost without exception, all the *magnifica* egg masses I've found, both in the wild and in my captive population, have been laid on the undersides of floating water lily leaves. This placement may allow the eggs to remain in water when pond levels drop.

Until recently, *magnifica* had a historic range that encompassed the entire lower Cape Fear River drainage, and possibly up into the Black River and Moores Creek drainages. That was its range until the past century; at one time within the past fifty years, it was abundant enough that it was collected for sale in the overseas aquarium pet trade.

The snail's preferred habitat appears to be old cypress ponds with mucky bottoms and a lot of water lilies. Unlike the ubiquitous marsh rams-horn, which can tolerate poor water quality and even some salt, the magnificent rams-horn is singularly sensitive to even trace levels of salt in its water, and most likely any trace of pollution. Because of its sensitivity, *magnifica* is now known to exist in only one old cypress pond in Brunswick County, though as recently as twenty years ago it was common in Greenfield Lake near downtown Wilmington.

If you talk to someone familiar with *Planorbella magnifica*, they will tell you it is a critically endangered species—

Magnificent rams-horn snail, *Planorbella magnifica*

possibly the most endangered mollusk in southeastern North Carolina. While *magnifica* is a North Carolina listed endangered species, it is not a federally-listed endangered species, at least not yet. This is partly in hopes of propagating genetically pure snails in captivity that can then be released into suitable ponds in the wild.

Ironically, if the snails are listed as federally endangered, they could be propagated in captivity, but if they carry the dubious label of "Endangered Species," landowners with suitable ponds may be less than welcome to the idea of having a listed animal reintroduced to their property. This conundrum is but one of the issues that makes the Endangered Species Act challenging for resource managers and landowners alike. And it is one reason why so many listed animals never get off the list—unless of course, they become extinct.

September Remembrance

SEPTEMBER 2001 September 12, 2001, was a somber day around the world, and I decided to begin it with a short walk through our backyard woods. I wasn't planning to go out in search of any one thing in particular. I walked slowly, listening to the early chattering of wrens and cardinals, and I was brought up short by a large web stretched across my path. A surprisingly small spider had made it: a lemon yellow beast called Micrathena. I regretted not seeing the web before wrapping my face and head in it, but I was able to secure its maker in the safety of a nearby shrub.

Extricating myself from the web, I soon found myself standing at the edge of the salt marsh that backed up to our wooded yard. The sun was still low on the horizon, and on everything there were dewdrops, the magic liquid that comes with cool autumn air. Looking out over the marsh, I saw countless spider webs, their gossamer forms catching the early rays of sunshine, dividing the light like prisms made of thread.

Soon, gentle breaths of morning air began to stir the dewy grass to movement. When one blade of grass bent to the breeze, another followed its lead, the two connected by a glinting strand of spider silk.

As the sun climbed higher above the horizon, the shapes and fantastic colors of those that made the webs were revealed. The iridescent red-and-silver-colored abdomen of a tiny orchard spider shone in the growing light as though illuminated from within, the spider's translucent green legs holding fast to the circular web as it billowed with the gathering breeze. The dancing rainbows cast from the spider's intricate work rivaled those produced by the finest crystals.

Before long, the delicate web was speckled with feathery seeds carried on the moving air from some near or distant plant. And then a small flying beetle, jet-black, with short, stout legs, was abruptly snatched by the sticky web. Too large to be held by such delicate fabric, the determined insect escaped, trailing a single thread from the base of one of its antennae. Now torn, and with more feathery seeds adorning it, the web was soon in need of repair, an effort the orchard spider attended to with mechanical precision.

In short order the rent created by the beetle was restored with new threadwork, the resulting patch clearly discernable from the original pattern, but no less functional. The spider ignored the seeds, but a tiny fly—possibly a flower-loving midge—was discovered ensnared in the web and trussed up for the daily larder.

The sunlight illuminated more webs in the leafy woodland behind me. They were much larger than the little orchard-spider variety seen in marsh grass. Spanning over two feet across, and composed of much heavier lines, these were the works of garden spiders, the robust black-and-yellow Argiope, of *Charlotte's Web* fame.

These webs also glinted in the early rays of sun, stretched across open spaces between trees and shrubs like fancy laceworks. Argiope spiders are early risers. They spin their trapping nets in the palest light, before daytime insects are active.

My only wish that morning was that I might have had younger eyes with me to witness what I had seen and felt. The simple act of watching dewdrops glisten on slender blades of grass is a healing elixir for troubled spirits, especially those of our children, many of whom are still struggling in the aftermath of September 11. And observing the delicate magic of a spider mending its web, nature restoring herself, provided a poignant metaphor to what still lies ahead for us, as our global population continues to try to rebuild a worldwide community of nations. In nature we find all the things we need for life, and in nature's magic we can find solace to help carry us through this day, and the promise of days to come.

Enviropolitics

SEPTEMBER 1992 I've decided the only way I can get through this quadrennial season of political discontent is by focusing my attention on the most important issue of the future: the environment.

Sadly, our species tends to ignore the fact that nothing in the political arena is of significant consequence without a healthy planet to stand it on. Humans are well adapted to respond to sudden dramatic events rather than subtle or protracted change. We can rally efforts to save communities ravaged by earthquakes, hurricanes, or tornadoes, but we aren't as good at charging to the rescue of a community suffering from chronic problems that bring about slow declines—problems like mercury in the water supply, pesticides in the soil, or carcinogens in the air. A fishing community hammered by a hurricane can be back in business in weeks, but when fish stocks that support that community gradually diminish because of overfishing, we lower our expectations and make do.

We've seen similar situations with logging communities and old-growth forests of the Pacific Northwest. Remember the northern spotted owl? You really shouldn't, because it's

not much of an owl—certainly not the sort of bird that war-
rants the public attention it received when the loggers felt
their livelihoods threatened by a reduction in the acreage of
old-growth forest allowable for logging. The logging industry,
which had sustained only a few generations of loggers,
became threatened not because of an owl in their midst, but
because the previous generations of loggers had cut close
to 95 percent of the old-growth forest that once supported
them. A gradual decline of available tree stocks was slowly,
almost imperceptibly, putting people out of work.

Alerted to the decline of native forests and the wildlife
they supported, biologists drew attention to the plight of
several native plant and wildlife species that depend on the
forests, including the now famous (or should I say infamous)
northern spotted owl. The biologists raised the alarm, sug-
gesting that the foresters were too late realizing their own
self-induced plight. But instead of admitting their mistake,
many loggers, with the help of misinformed politicians,
chose an innocuous owl as a scapegoat for the sorry state
of affairs brought about by selfish and shortsighted forest
management policies.

All the while, as politicians vied with environmentalists
and loggers for media time, the trees continued to fall until
finally it was clear that there just weren't enough trees to go
around, and for the residents to survive, communities would
either have to diversify their economic base of operations, or
move. Sadly, we didn't learn much from this experience. The
loggers were going to go out of business regardless of any
owl—because the resource that once buoyed their economy
had been depleted beyond sustainability.

Some pollsters report that Americans consider the environment their number four or five most important political

concern, following health care, taxes, the economy, and other environmentally dependent issues. In today's political climate, environmental issues are lost as background noise—largely ignored until a crisis thunders loudly. The assumption that we can sustain a healthy economy while the environment dwindles away is severely myopic, and a disservice to future generations. There is no issue in any agenda more critically important to our species than the health and well-being of our environment.

Ecology and economics deal with the same root, *ecos*, which is Greek for "home"; ecology deals with the study of the home, and economics deals with the management of the home. So when you hear talk during this political season about economics, remember, in the final analysis, it's really the health and well-being of the environment that determines the health of our economy.

Wildlife Management

SEPTEMBER 1994 Over the next few weeks, the North Carolina Wildlife Resources Commission has scheduled public hearings concerning the protection of the state's non-game and endangered animals. For a long time now, I have tried to give voice for the many little, and often unsung, animals and plants that too often go overlooked by wildlife managers.

As a student in college majoring in wildlife management, I would often find myself at odds with the old-school "wildlifers" who focused their attention on a select handful of wildlife game species. At the time, non-game wildlife was at best an afterthought; their needs were considered only after those of the "game" species had been fully explored. These include white-tailed deer, bobwhite quail, mourning dove, largemouth bass, gray squirrel, and cottontail rabbit. Wild turkey and numerous kinds of ducks were also counted among this elite group of intently managed wildlife, but not counted among them were the hundreds of other species of so-called non-game wildlife—the animals not sought for sport or food. The list of non-game species is too long to begin here, but suffice it to say it includes animals deserving of no less consideration than deer or quail.

My concern in college for non-game animals was encouraged by a handful of likeminded wildlife management co-students. We'd often get together after class lectures and lament to one another about how tired we each were with deer and turkey facts, or dove and bass requirements. Occasionally in class, one or more of us would question our mentors about the future of non-game management, but the discussions that followed never seemed to last long, and soon the lecture would return once again to the relative virtues of one game species or another.

Of course game species management does benefit non-game species. But in wildlife management, the needs of non-game species are considered secondary. Monies for wildlife management are usually allocated to those species that can show the disbursing agency some form of return, preferably monetary. This comes typically from hunting and fishing license fees and other funds.

During my last semesters in college, the issue of non-game wildlife management became more than a side topic of discussion. In time, non-game wildlife management courses were even developed; the reason for this sudden turn of events was, of course, money. Some visionary scientist figured out a way to place a monetary figure on the intrinsic value of a wild animal that isn't harvested or sold. "Non-consumptive species," they first called them, and the formulas used to evaluate them incorporated such factors as photography-related revenues and travel revenues generated from wildlife tourism (they were later called "watchable wildlife").

Measuring the tangible versus intangible values of wildlife usually comes down to the matter of potential financial return that each promises for our society. A hunter's dead deer is worth X dollars—that much can be easily determined. But how much is a live box turtle or woodpecker worth? Formulas are now being developed to agree on the intrinsic, intangible, non-consumptive wildlife value for these little guys, but it still comes down to a question of dollars and cents.

We are all familiar with the old adage, "art for art's sake." To me this implies that art, consumptive or otherwise, is intrinsically valuable. Well, I propose we adopt the adage, wildlife for wildlife's sake. But lest my proposal be too easily dismissed, let me add that it's for our sake as well.

Wildlife management involves much more than just hunting and fishing. It should be steered by ecological principles. Too often we manage our resources, including wildlife, not by principle, but by public pressure and political whim, neither of which have much to do with ecology. For too long we have failed to appreciate the fact that all life on Earth, each and every species of plant and animal, is interwoven with one another. For this reason I believe the term wildlife should be used in an inclusive context which enjoins game species, non-game species, and to some extent, even our own species. That way, when we manage for one species using ecological principles as our guide, we will be managing for ourselves.

To Hibernate or Not

SEPTEMBER 1991 This is a tough time of year to be a turtle. I try to imagine being in a turtle's shell when the autumn weather gets fickle—warm and sunny one day, frigid, cold, and rainy the next. For a creature whose body temperature sways with the whims of weather, this means cold weather can very quickly slow down your movements and your thoughts, which, for a turtle, are none too rapid to begin with. Premeditated intellect is not a turtle's strong point. That's not to imply that turtles aren't bright; indeed, turtles are pretty sharp as reptiles go, as evidenced by the fact that they have been around since before the age of dinosaurs.

But even though temperate-zone turtles have a long history that includes changing seasons, each autumn this enduring group of animals must decide when to hunker down and dig a burrow to shut down in for the winter.

For a turtle, there is a lot more riding on this decision than there is for us when we debate whether to take our coat with us when we leave the house in the morning. A turtle needs to consume calorie-rich foods up to the last minute before taking a winter hiatus, so a quick drop in temperature during the day—almost guaranteed to happen at least once during the fall—can bring fatal consequences if the turtle is caught unaware.

One turtle in particular, the box turtle, is notably sensitive to sudden downturns of temperature, because this land-based turtle, which usually buries itself under logs or leaves on the forest floor for winter, can suffer frostbite and worse if exposed to freezing air. If a box turtle is caught out on a warm, sunny day and a high pressure cold-front suddenly bears down from the north, the cold-stunned turtle may not be able to move fast enough to re-bury itself in its winter lair. And the faster the temperature drops, the slower the turtle can react to the change.

Water turtles, including pond sliders and snapping turtles, are a little less susceptible to cold-front changes than land turtles are, because water cools more slowly than air. A pond turtle caught basking on a log when a cold front arrives has only to plop into the water and nuzzle itself into the fluffy ooze on the pond bottom. Once settled in, most aquatic turtles can slow down their metabolism and extract enough oxygen from water to feed their brain and other essential organs. This is accomplished by blood vessel-rich tissue in the turtle's mouth, throat, and cloaca . . . but I digress.

I've seen box turtles hiding in water to escape the cold, but unlike true aquatic turtles, the more terrestrially oriented box turtle runs the risk of drowning or catching a cold that could quickly lead to respiratory pneumonia. The box turtle's life is fraught with autumn choices.

Lizards, too, have to make a similar climatic decision. Because lizards are less bulky, they warm up and cool down more quickly than turtles. Although they are faster on their feet, you're still likely to find lizards close to their cold-weather refuge this time of year. Lizards can emerge even in February, a very un-reptilian time of year, but usually they are on top of log piles or other sheltered havens in which they've been spending winter's cold days and colder nights. I can't count the times I've accidentally disturbed the slumber of some innocent lizard by overturning a log, plant pot, or other sheltering object in my back yard. The common Carolina anole, or chameleon as most people know it, uses its color to help adjust to temperature. On hot days, the anole turns bright green to reflect the heat of the sun. On cool, cloudy days this lizard turns dark brown to absorb more heat from the sun's rays. In the dead of winter, some of these lizards appear to be nearly black, and when I turn up one of that color, I feel guilty for having further exposed it to the cold.

As autumn grows into winter this year, the road-rescued box turtles in the outdoor pen I constructed are now debating whether to call it a summer. I loosened the soil in one corner of their enclosure to enable them to burrow down out of winter's way. To help aerate the soil I mixed in a basket of small crape myrtle leaves. Once the turtles show they've decided to retire for winter, I will cover them with another layer of leaves, add a layer of humus-rich soil, and then top it off with a thick blanket of pine straw and oak leaves.

I have to make the right decision about when to do this, because unseasonably warm late-autumn weather may draw the turtles out from under their thermal blanket, thus exposing them to the inevitable chill that will follow. But if I do judge properly, the turtles will stay snuggled in their protective burrow of leaves and soil, through the winter cold, insulated from frost and harm. If the turtles stay put as they should, we won't see each other again until around

April, when warm spring days heat the soil and stimulate the turtle's annual awakening. Now isn't that something to look forward to, as we await the arrival of winter?

Flytrap Lament

OCTOBER 2000 When I first heard that a scout troop was going to move some Venus' flytraps from the footprint of a proposed county project, my first thought was one of gratitude for the troop and its leaders. My second thought conjured a question: Where were they going to put the habitat-dependent transplants?

In the wild, the Venus' flytrap is an inconspicuous, flowering perennial plant that grows low to the ground, its bright green leaves radiating out from a central onionlike root base. Each leaf may grow to four or five inches long, and in the wild, this rare plant's only conspicuous feature is its delicate white flowers, which bloom in May. The Venus' flytrap is called carnivorous because it traps small insects by means of uniquely modified pads at the end of each leaf. Annual pads increase in size as the plant ages, and with older plants, the one-inch-long pads are capable of closing like a miniature bear trap on insects as large as bees. The pads are sometimes brilliant red on the inside surface, a coloring that may serve to attract certain insects. Along the pads' outer edge are numerous short spines that act like bars on a jail cell as the pads close over their prey, thus preventing escape.

On the inner surface of each pad are three barely visible trigger hairs that, when stimulated by the movement of an insect, cause an electrical current to run through the trap to the leaf's midline, prompting cells in the pad hinge to immediately lengthen. This rapid cell growth causes the pads to fold over in less than a second and embrace whatever triggered the hairs—not a sentient reaction as with a hawk clutching a mouse, but marvelously effective nonetheless. And like the hawk, the flytrap captures animal prey for a singular purpose: nourishment.

Flytraps, pitcher plants, sundews, butterworts, and many other so-called carnivorous plants perform their carnivory because the medium in which they grow lacks the essential nutrients the plants require, most notably the element nitrogen. Flytraps in particular typically grow in acidic peat moss soils, the decomposed remains of a spongy green moss called sphagnum. Soils such as those found in very specific wetland habitats in or near longleaf-pine savannas are the flytrap's only natural habitat. Here, pine straw rains down to the ground, adding acid that suppresses nitrogen-fixing bacteria in the organic soil.

Without bacteria to convert nitrogen in the soil, carnivorous plants ingeniously capture and digest free-roaming packets of nitrogen, otherwise known as insects. Flies, wasps, ants, and beetles are nothing more than fertilizer to the flytrap.

After the insect is captured by the stealthy plant, its soft parts are digested with enzymes secreted by special glandlike cells in the plant's leaf wall. Once liquefied, the insect's good stuff, nitrogen, is then absorbed through the leaf wall—another amazing ability, considering that most plants absorb nutrients through their roots. After digestion,

Venus' flytrap, *Dionaea musciplua*

all that remains of the insect prey is the dried husk of its outer skeleton. It's a grisly process to say the least, and one that each individual leaf may perform up to three times.

In their wild habitats, flytraps grow amid a plush green carpet of sphagnum moss that belies many generations of dead, brown peat beneath this lively countenance: generations of mosses and other plants dating back centuries in young habitats, millennia in older. And of even greater significance than the age of the flytrap's habitat is the fact that southeastern North Carolina is the only place in the world where Venus' flytrap grows in the wild. The *only* place. Sadly, it is a plant imperiled in the wild in large part due to habitat alteration and loss. And because flytraps require such specific growing conditions, they cannot be planted just anyplace and expected to survive, let alone thrive.

Flytraps are protected by North Carolina state law from collecting without a permit. Ironically they do not enjoy protection from bulldozers, and it is largely for this reason that the flytrap and its wondrous habitats are disappearing from the wild. Sure, we can preserve the species in captivity, just as we do rare tigers. We can find flytraps for sale in supermarkets because they, like tigers, can be propagated in captivity. But what good is there in a captive tiger if its species has no place left in the wild? Part of what makes a species a species is the place it lives. And just as tigers deserve their place in the wild to be a species in their own right, flytraps do too. And herein lays the conundrum for a well-meaning scout troop trying to help a rare species: where to put a plant that is rapidly becoming a stranger in its own strange land?

Salt Marsh Raptor

OCTOBER 1999 I was wandering around an open expanse of salt marsh behind the North Carolina Aquarium recently when my attention was caught by the sight of a large bird flying overhead. I recognized the animal as an osprey, known also as the fish hawk because of its preference for fishy prey. Ospreys belong to the group of predatory birds called raptors. True raptors include eagles, hawks, falcons, vultures, and owls. The group is often referred to as "birds of prey," but I believe this term is too inclusive to reserve for the raptors alone—a lot of other birds, including such common songbirds as bluebirds and robins, prey on animals. A bluebird will dispatch a large grasshopper by bashing the poor insect against a branch, an act that surely should earn it the title "bird of prey"!

The name *raptor* has long been translated to mean "thief." I prefer to think the name refers to the unique feet this group possesses: raptorial or grasping feet designed for grabbing prey (except for the vultures, who have feet that can hold down dead animals to expedite the process of pulling their flesh off). The osprey's feet almost epitomize the term *raptorial* because their four toes are exceptionally strong, tipped with needle-sharp talons, and each foot's pads are rough and scaly to help grip slippery fish, the osprey's primary quarry.

More typical raptors, such as the red-tailed hawks we see along roadsides, make their living hunting mice and other small prey. Their keen eyesight can discern a mouse at several hundred feet, and, swooping in low and fast, they're able to snag the intended meal, at least one time for every ten attempts. That's about the same odds as a lion pursuing its quarry.

Not so the osprey. Not only do ospreys feed almost exclusively on fish rather than mice, but they also have a much better hunting average, with a successful capture occurring about once in every four or five attempts. This is a remarkable statistic, considering the osprey is looking down on its prey, often from a distance of a hundred feet or more, and because the prey is under the water's surface, the osprey must account for the bending of light that causes images to shift position underwater.

The osprey working the marsh creek this day entertained me with a classic osprey performance. As it coursed over the marsh creek, the bird checked its flight mid-wingbeat, stalled briefly, then plunged headlong for the water. Even from my vantage point a couple hundred feet away, I could sense the determined intent in the bird's actions.

Ospreys dive with their head and feet thrust forward and their wings swept back. It's a bizarre sight because their head is tucked between their feet, toes extended and ready to clutch. Then, at the instant before hitting the water, the osprey pivots its head and body back, so that its feet enter the water first, ideally striking prey in the process. The momentum from the dive is so great that the bird usually gets a complete dunking before lifting itself out of the water. Once airborne, the osprey adjusts its catch so that it flies with the fish oriented aerodynamically, head forward. Once it has secured its grip on the fish and has gained secure altitude above the water, the osprey rouses itself, the bird's equivalent of a dog shaking dry. All of this occurs in a matter of a few short seconds from the time it strikes the water. It is truly a sight that evokes a sense of respect for an animal's skill and ability.

The idea that raptors are little more than thieves seems like a cheap and undeserved stereotype. Witnessing this osprey perform its successful aerial display, I saw a more fitting definition for the title raptor. It comes from the word *rapt,* meaning "lifted up and carried away."

Red Tide

The cool days of November are traditionally the best days for shellfishing in our area. This year, however, a big change has occurred in shellfish populations, due to one very small organism.

Red tide, or in North Carolina more of a yellow tide, has appeared and disrupted an intricate web of life that touches almost every coastal animal. This red tide, as the phenomenon has been titled, is not actually a tide at all, but rather a conglomerate of millions upon millions of floating plantlike animals called dinoflagellate, though some might say they're animal-like plants. Either way, these microscopic organisms occur naturally in our offshore marine waters, but in North Carolina they rarely overpopulate and become a nuisance in shellfishing waters.

Dinoflagellates come in an assortment of shapes and colors. Most are oval in shape and possess two long appendages known as flagellum that wave and beat about, providing some limited locomotion. The most common colors of these less-than-tiny organisms are green and red.

Normally, the dinoflagellate population is held in check by a number of factors, including water temperature and the presence of slightly larger organisms that feed on them. Cooler waters inhibit reproduction, and so when water temperatures rise above normal or when the water stays unusually warm during cooler months, the balance of nature is thrown off quite a bit.

Dinoflagellates often congregate in offshore waters where ocean upwelling brings bottom nutrients to the surface, where more sunshine is present to help the dinoflagellates multiply. Red-tide dinoflagellates are seen inshore, especially in the Gulf of Mexico, where they bloom almost every year in the warm, nutrient-rich waters there. Our coastal waters in North Carolina don't often support this kind of annual event, but there is some belief among many researchers that too many nutrients in marine sediments along our coast can promote an overpopulation of marine microorganisms, including the poorly understood dinoflagellate.

While it is not fully known why the dinoflaggelates are toxic, we do know *how* they are toxic. One dinoflagellate by itself is not too noxious, but when combined in a mass numbering of hundreds of millions or even billions, the tiny amount of toxin each one produces is multiplied accordingly, with sometimes devastating results. The toxin they produce is a type of alkaloid, a chemical compound found in a variety of plants and animals, including some mushrooms and several kinds of amphibians. Alkaloids cause a burning sensation to our eyes and mucous membranes because they literally react with these sensitive tissues, causing them to dissolve slightly.

Now, in order to understand why shellfishing is so easily affected by the red tide we need only look at how clams, oysters, and other bivalves (two-shelled mollusks) eat. They breathe oxygen from water through siphons, and in the process they extract suspended bits of food directly from the water by means of netlike filters. When the population of dinoflagellates increases, the shellfish can concentrate the alkaloid in their body tissue, maybe not enough to harm themselves, but possibly enough to cause severe illness to any animal that tries to eat them.

This year's red tide is a warning signal to us: it's telling us something is wrong with our coastal waters. And the repeated shellfish area closings that occur in our area even in the absence of red tides tell us something is wrong with our community. Remember, shellfish area closings due to red tide are usually brief. But shellfish areas closed because of polluted stormwater runoff from development will be closed for a long, long time. But maybe that's something we can wait for our children to fix.

Thanksgiving Thanks

NOVEMBER 1988 A hardwood forest in November is a fine place to relax and think about Thanksgiving. In our area, this is the time of plenty, and the animals show it. While I often wonder how much fun it would be to transform myself into an animal, I find this thought coming most frequently in November. I think this is because when I look around the woods, I see much that appears edible, at least to something other than me.

Even on a cool, wet November day when it's overcast and dark, I can find something that is reveling in the weather. This type of day is for the black-and-silver-colored marbled salamanders. These portly, moist-skinned amphibians have kept themselves burrowed underground throughout the dry heat of summer, and now they can once again come out from their hiding places. A cool, wet day is perfect for the salamanders because they need not fear snakes and turtles, for these threats are now hunkered down to escape winter's approach. Perfect, also, because the salamander's favorite food, the earthworm, can be easily found among the forest's leaf litter and moss. I envy the marbled salamander on a day like this—few enemies, plenty of worms to eat, and cool, damp moss to crawl upon.

Just above the forest floor, in the region known as the forest understory, we find the home of numerous insects and spiders year round. However, during the cool days of November, these cold-sensitive invertebrates are sluggish and hence vulnerable to the sharp eyes of colorful warblers and other insect-eating birds. If you have ever spent time watching a warbler, you already know that they are never motionless, and they have an uncanny ability to place a branch between themselves and anything trying to observe them. These little winged forest gnomes are also insatiably curious. They investigate every strand of spider web strung between the smallest branches, and every crack and crevice and loose piece of bark on every tree in the forest, all the while shielding themselves from view. My envy for warblers is that they probably see more species of spiders in one day than a good entomologist finds in a month. Even though it's Thanksgiving, I would have a hard time eating some of the jumping spiders the warblers find. Not because these spiders are unattractive—but because they have such appealing personalities, compared to many of the other woodland spiders I know.

Towering above the forest understory, in the canopy, you can find a unique and shy creature known as the flying squirrel. Flying squirrels do not truly fly; rather, they glide, usually from tree to tree or branch to branch. They hide and sleep by day in abandoned woodpecker holes high above the ground, and as the sun sets they poke their inquisitive noses out from their sleeping quarters, test the air for the scent of enemies, and, detecting none, suddenly launch themselves into space. Loose folds of skin stretched between their limbs give them a kitelike ability, trapping air to provide lift while their huge black eyes and twitching nose scan the surrounding canopy for signs of food or danger.

November is the time for acorns and berries, and so it would be a good time to be a flying squirrel. The thorny greenbrier's black berries, the oak tree's acorns, and the forest floor's mushrooms provide the flying squirrel with a banquet that surely can't be beat. And if the opportunity presents itself, a flying squirrel will not pass up a little extra protein in the form of a sleeping cricket or juicy beetle grub.

Looking around a November forest, I see woodland animals having their own Thanksgiving meals, and even though the food may not be served from fancy plates placed on smooth wooden tables, I am certain the salamanders, warblers, and flying squirrels would agree that their place settings could not be finer.

Snow Seeds

November 1995 It's November on the coast and already it has begun to snow. Not real snowflakes, mind you, but the downy seeds of the baccharis plant are blowing around like a blizzard. Baccharis, also called groundsel tree, is a common shrub along our coastline. It inhabits that fine line area bordering salt marshes where the high-tide salt water just reaches, but doesn't inundate them.

I highlight baccharis at this time of year because the fluffy clouds of seeds a baccharis shrub produces are a measurable tick on our annual clock of seasons. Just as the change of color in red maple leaves tells us early autumn has arrived, the baccharis seed clouds tell us we are entering late autumn. Right now, with the first real wave of cold air from the north behind us, we are entering a time of dormancy and change. Already gone from our scene are the warm-weather friends the lizards and turtles. One or two may pop out when the sun warms us up for a few consecutive days, but, for the most part, cold-blooded animals are now lying low, getting ready for the long wait until spring.

When the baccharis seeds are carried on the wind, we can expect fiddler crabs to burrow down deep into the marsh soil, to escape the inevitable coming of cold weather. Gone from the marsh flats are the telltale fiddler crab signs: the little BB-sized pellets of sand they produce while feeding, and the marble-sized globs the busy crabs bring to the marsh surface while excavating their tunnels. Gone too are the crabs' finger-sized tunnel entrances that pockmark the marsh during warm months. The plumed baccharis seeds, which so resemble downy feathers or snow, blow over a less animated marsh when the fiddlers disappear.

The seed plumes are not lost, though. The hispid cotton rat, a furry little rodent that also lives in the marsh, gathers the seed to line its winter quarters as insulation against the chill. And if conditions prove favorable, perhaps a new generation of baccharis will take hold where the cotton rat inadvertently set seed.

Following a cloud of seeds back to their origin usually provides a chance to see how, in other ways, baccharis benefits residents of the marsh. Strung between the coarse-textured baccharis stems are the remnants of spider webs, though now these webs are tattered and clogged with the ever-present seed plumes. On close examination, a thumb-sized egg case may be seen hanging within the tangle of webbing and seeds. The most common large spider-egg case in the marsh comes from the black-and-yellow Argiope spider, though by now the animal that produced the egg case is gone, having spent her brief life securing the promise for a next generation—a promise maybe more greatly secured with each insulating baccharis seed plume the web snatches. Eventually, and I suppose ideally, the whole mess—web, egg case, and seed plumes—will become a ball of the finest insulation nature can provide.

Groundsel tree, *Baccharis halimifolia*

Come spring—and I am already looking forward to it—the spiderlings that wintered in their insulated ball of fluff will emerge, probably around the same time the baccharis leaves begin to sprout. The fiddler crabs will crawl out from their winter tunnels in the marsh flats, and at once, a promise of life in the marsh begins anew.

On the Wing

NOVEMBER 2000 To many songbirds, North Carolina is just one leg of an annual journey. For some, the journey begins in the northeastern part of the continent, and it may span as far south as Ecuador. Some songbirds, weighing less than an ounce or two, will follow a path more than four thousand miles long—and that's just to get to their winter grounds. They repeat the trip in spring with a northbound journey back to their summer breeding grounds, a mystifying accomplishment, considering that many of these birds— cardinals, orioles, and sparrows—weigh about the equivalent of a chicken egg.

Many of the birds power-fly for hours on end, even flapping nonstop from dawn to dusk when there's a tailwind blowing. Their habit of flying in the dark is beneficial because fewer predators are on the wing at night, aside from the odd owl here and there. The songbirds can be heard chattering back and forth to one another as they wing overhead, an instinct that helps them stay close together in the dark. And in addition to flying with the wind, the birds often rotate turns flying in one another's slipstream in order to conserve energy.

When it's time to recharge, the diminutive songbirds

settle down in whichever leg of the trip they get to. In this way, the trip is divided into sections. Most birds have this ingrained in their biological makeup, and don't think about the trip as we might; they travel where the weather and food carry them, and in so doing, they cover considerable distances with each nightly hopover. Nonetheless, for songbirds, migration is a perilous trip. They have to find shelter, food, and water, while staying vigilant, lest they fall prey to some stealthy predator, be it a sharp-shinned hawk, a screech owl, or a house cat.

This year is no exception to the songbirds' routine travel, and right now is when their game nears its peak, where wins are awarded just for surviving. It is no small fact that southeastern North Carolina, with its bottomland swamps, evergreen shrub thickets, and longleaf-pine woodlands, is very important to songbirds. These habitats are what the birds need most when they reach this leg of their trip. They will settle in the shelter of the trees each morning and feast on the nourishing bounty of berries, seeds, and insects found amid tangled-up twigs and branches. The little birds will gorge themselves in order to power up for the continued flight south, and to insulate themselves against the cold winds and nights they'll experience if inclement weather forces them to stay around, as many have had to do during this chilly autumn.

Having been spared the fruit-stripping winds of a hurricane this year, many trees and shrubs bear an abundant supply of seeds and berries, upon which countless birds are right now drawing sustenance. Later, during their southward migration, the birds will pass the seeds they gulped down during their brief stopover. Of course, this is how birds and plants have been connected for countless generations; the plants supply energy to the birds, which they then use to power their flight, carrying with them the seeds of a new generation of plants. In so doing, the birds enable the trees and shrubs to expand their genetic range to other communities farther south along their migration route.

So, in a sense, we are connected to the rest of the world by the energy transmitted through birds and trees. This is one more reason why we should protect and restore the natural ecosystems we have here, especially our older forests. For without these places, we risk breaking an integral circuit of life that right now, we can hear and see, winging high overhead.